J.U. Stice 2/16/02

SAINTLY AND CELESTIAL PROPHECIES OF JOY AND RENEWAL

REVELATIONS FOR A NEW MILLENNIUM

ANDREW RAMER

D0949328

HarperSanFrancisco

An Imprint of HarperCollins*Publishers*

For my mother, Gerry. *Peering at the crocuses in snow through a frosty window.*

My father, Jack. *On tiptoes, watching you paint.*

Erick Faigin, *who led me to the path but did not stay to walk it with me.*

And Isaac Kikawada. *You taught me how to hear the outer voices that allowed me to turn inward.*

With endless gratitude.

Grateful acknowledgment is made for permission to reproduce the skull diagrams on page 82, from *Clinical Anatomy Made Ridiculously Simple* by Stephen Goldberg, Medmaster, 1991.

Skeletal diagrams on page 76 are from *Art Students' Anatomy* by Edmond J. Farris, Dover Publications, Inc. Used with permission.

A TREE CLAUSE BOOK

HarperSanFrancisco and the author, in association with The Basic Foundation, a not-for-profit organization whose primary mission is reforestation, will facilitate the planting of two trees for every one tree used in the manufacture of this book.

REVELATIONS FOR A NEW MILLENNIUM: *Saintly and Celestial Prophecies of Joy and Renewal.* Copyright © 1997 by Andrew Ramer. All rights reserved. Printed in the United States of America. No part of this book may be used or reproduced in any manner whatsoever without written permission except in the case of brief quotations embodied in critical articles and reviews. For information address HarperCollins Publishers, 10 East 53rd Street, New York, NY 10022.

HarperCollins Web Site: http://www.harpercollins.com
HarperCollins®, ⬛®, HarperSanFrancisco™, and A TREE CLAUSE BOOK®
are trademarks of HarperCollins Publishers Inc.

FIRST EDITION

Library of Congress Cataloging-in-Publication Data
Ramer, Andrew.
Revelations for a new millennium : saintly and celestial prophecies of joy and renewal / Andrew Ramer.
ISBN 0–06–251470–9 (pbk.)
1. Spirit writings. 2. Private revelations. 3. Angels—Miscellanea. 4. Ramer, Andrew. 5. Spiritual life. I. Title.
BG1301.R215   1997
133.9'3—dc20   96–36515

97 98 99 00 01 ❖ RRDH 10 9 8 7 6 5 4 3 2 1

Contents

PART THREE
LIVING IN A WORLD OF ORDINARY SPLENDORS

Contents

Acknowledgments

Books are created in community. In addition to thanking the true authors of this work, whose scribe I am, I would like to acknowledge the following:

The many listeners, known and unknown, of the world scriptures that are the deep foundation for my own listening.

My partner Randy Higgins, Richard Ramer, Kate Shepherd, Lucy Dratler, and the rest of my family. Joy Manesiotis, Chris Beach, Zoë Beach, Barbara Shor, Nelson Bloncourt, Don Shewey, Lynne Reynolds, John Stowe, Jeanne Spiegel, Steve Zipperstein, Michael Friedman, for anchoring me in the world. And Howard Morhaim, my agent, for his focus, clarity, and continual support.

Houston Wood, Selma Weiner, Rabbi Fox, for their guidance. Cheryl Woodruff, for starting me off so well. Kevin Flodd and Carol Robin, for tuning me into bones. Bonnie Gintis, for helping me weave sound and science together in Chapter Six. Linda Sherwood, Jane Roberts, Harriet Goldman, Donna Cunningham, Alma Daniel, Timothy

Wyllie, for listening too. Virginia, Pamela, David, Israel, and everyone else at Mail Boxes Etc.

Being at Harper San Francisco is like coming home. I want to thank everyone there who has worked with me on this book, especially my editor, Kevin Bentley. His enthusiasm, support, and vision are what every writer dreams of. With deep gratitude and joy. Thank you all!

Acknowledgments

Introduction

The stories that a people tell are the container that holds their world together and gives meaning to their lives. We have entered a new era in our history. It began near Alamogordo, New Mexico, on 16 July 1945, when the first atomic bomb exploded. As we face a new millennium, it is time for us to tell new stories, stories that reflect our capacity for destruction and our ability to reach the stars. Stories that reflect our emerging global culture, that acknowledge our deepest dreams.

I am a storyteller. My stories rise up from the depths of my soul, and like the work of any artist, they belong to everyone. They are not even my own stories, for all of them are stories that have been told to me, that I pass on to you.

Since I was a child I have heard voices—of God, of angels. I think all children do. When I was small, that was considered cute, but as I got older I discovered that grown-ups didn't hear voices, and didn't want to hear about mine. So I stopped talking about them—but they did not go away. For years I thought I was the only one who heard voices. Then I found out about Joan of Arc, and I was both comforted and terrified, comforted that she too had heard voices, and terrified—by her fate. But I discovered that if I sang to myself very loudly I could block out the voices. This magic worked by day, but I was powerless at night, when voices would continue to talk to me in my sleep. Often I thought that I was going crazy, but I never told anyone, and got better and better at not listening—to the voices, or, over time, to myself.

No matter what I did, the voices never went away. It wasn't till I was in college that I began to wonder if they might be not threats, but friendly. In 1969 or '70 I decided that I would listen to them for six months as an experiment. I called it "trusting my intuition." Nothing awful happened. On the contrary, my life seemed more balanced. The voices brought simple messages: do this, go here, eat that. Nothing strange or frightening. Then, in 1971, when I was living in Jerusalem, God started talking to me again. I moved between awe, exhilaration, and fear. Finally, the only friend I told sent me off to see a rabbi, who said I would go crazy if I didn't stop listening, that I needed to be grounded in the world before I did anything else.

After that meeting, for the first time in my life, the voices stopped. I finished college, with a degree in religious studies from the University of California at Berkeley, moved to New York, and got a job in a bookstore. And it was only in 1976, when my life was grounded and settled, that the voices began again, at first as only a quiet whisper. In the beginning they were ordinary voices, like friends on the telephone. It was only after I got used to them that they started talking to me about healing, about our history, about planetary transformation.

In those days we called the voices guides, spirit guides. It is clear to me now that they aren't guides so much as saints. They came in wave after wave, first saints and angels, and then God again, as both Mother and Father. The voices have been a healing for me, a gift and a blessing. Over the years I've filled countless journals, notebooks, and computer disks with the words they've dictated to me.

Many of us hear voices. I know—from the people I've met in the workshops I've led, from the letters my writing partners and I have received, from *Angel Answers* and *Ask Your Angels,* which I authored and co-authored, from people thanking us for letting them know that they are not the only ones who talk to angels or to God. But if you do not hear voices, how can I describe to you what it's like? Actually, it's not very different from picking up the phone when it rings. A voice is there. It fills my brain. In an instant I know if it is a familiar voice or a new one. Only there is no external listening device. All the sound is inside my head, as loud and clear as a good phone connection. Each voice has its own tone, its own vibration. I can always tell if it's a saint or an angel I'm talking to. They vibrate differently. And on those rare occasions when God talks, there is no doubt about who's there, for the voice doesn't just glow in the back of my brain, but fills my entire body, resonant and golden. And except for their initial appearances, which are often unexpected, I always know when the phone is ringing, and I always have the right to let it keep ringing, or to pick it up and say, "Hi, I'm busy now. Could you call back later?" And they always do.

Over the years I've asked my invisible teachers again and again where they are and how their voices get inside my head. They've always answered in the same way—that they exist in a plane of reality that coexists with our own. And that I hear their voices "broadcast" into my head somewhat the same way that I hear a radio when I turn it on, its voices beamed out from a tower a distance away, but filling the air for miles in every direction with invisible waves.

I was finishing a novel when the angels suggested that I go through more than twelve years of notebooks, journals, and computer disks and put together the messages that hadn't gone into *Angel Answers.* It had never occurred to me to do that, and it seemed an overwhelming task. But just as with *Angel Answers,* midway into the project of typing things into my computer, I realized that "they" had been planning this book all along. Everything fit effortlessly into place, with a few revisions here and there from one or two of them. My own work is slow. I've been struggling with my novel for almost twenty years. But their work is easy. In three weeks I'd put together years of messages into the book you're about to read. And it is that level of co-creation that they are inviting us all

to participate in, on a global level, as we move toward the next
millennium.

✳   ✳   ✳

This book is a collection of messages from many different voices.
I call them revelations, and I think of them in that way. But it's
also important to put the word *revelations* in perspective. We are
fourfold beings, with physical, mental, emotional, and spiritual
aspects. Each of us has different talents, abilities, and skills, and
we all excel in different areas. I cannot dribble a basketball, drive
a car, restrain myself from throwing dishes when I get angry,
play anything but the black keys on a piano, or fix a broken toilet.
But I can listen to voices. Three millennia ago, people who did
that were considered holy. Increasingly over the last two millennia, people who did that were considered crazy. To me, it's simply
about what we're good at. The more balanced we become in all
four aspects, the less we will need to elevate (or eliminate) people
whose area of expertise is spiritual. In the future, a car mechanic
will be celebrated in the same way as a prophet, an athlete, a
scholar, a parent, a farmer, a secretary, a firefighter, a letter carrier.
More than anyone I feel like Julia Child. She's spent years in the
bustle of her kitchen, preparing different kinds of food, creating
recipes to feed the body—while I have spent years in the silence
of my room, listening to my still, small voices, preparing recipes
to feed the soul.

There are three parts to this book. The first, "The Roots of
Our Rich History," describes the human journey from its start
until the present. It does not begin with Eden but millions of
years ago, and its perspective is not just local but also galactic, a
story large enough for the world that we now live in. In addition
to history, you will be meeting a gathering of unknown saints that
you yourself can open to, for wisdom and comfort and guidance.
Each chapter in this section comes from a different source, and
each chapter has its own introduction that will present you to the
speakers whose scribe I have been.

On our journey to a new millennium we all must learn to anchor what we've learned in the physical world, not just on the

mental or spiritual plane. In part 2, "Grounding Wisdom in Your Body and Your Life," you will find a very specific technique from saints and angels that will allow you to awaken to the wisdom that you carry within your own body, deep within your bones, so that you can be the source of your own revelations. Then you will find a ten-step path to explore, a guided journey of transformation given to us by the angels. That is followed by a short section on conscious dying, for death is a part of life, not something to be feared.

Part 3, "Living in a World of Ordinary Splendors," begins with a collection of messages from different angels, on subjects ranging from evil to creative manifestation. These passages offer guidance, inspiration, and practical tools for living in a new era, a new millennium. They will help you to be conscious of your own spiritual journey, and will support you in seeing yourself as both a resident of Planet Earth and a citizen of our entire universe. The book ends with the messages I have received from God over the past few years, messages of comfort and wisdom for living on earth in a new and radiant way.

This is a book of revelations. Today not everyone hears voices, not everyone is open to the inflow of cosmic consciousness. But in the future, all of us will be open in this way, all of us will be prophets and sibyls. Today these messages may seem like madness or like miracles. But the angels tell me that anyone who listens is a perfectly ordinary person—for a hundred years from now. They tell me that we are moving toward a time when all of us will be open to saints, angels, and God. Then we will not need anyone else to tell us how to live our lives, any more than we will need someone else to fix our stove. For all of us will be living in balance, harmony, and connection. And it is for that world and for that time and for that way of living as embodied souls that this book has been created. With blessings to you, its readers, on the journey toward joy and renewal, on the journey to the next one thousand years.

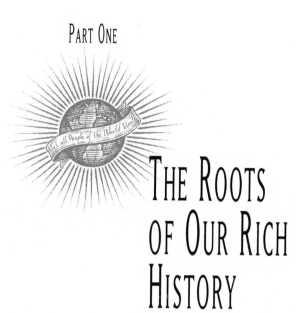

PART ONE

THE ROOTS
OF OUR RICH
HISTORY

Chapter 1

THE STORY OF WHO WE ARE

 ince 1976 I'd been listening to my inner voices and recording their messages. The speakers were saints, human teachers no longer focused in the physical world. You'll meet them later in this section. It wasn't until the spring of 1982 that the angels entered my life. One night I was sitting on my bedroom floor, meditating, when a shimmer appeared in the wall I was facing. The shimmer turned into a face, and then an angel emerged from that face and stood beside me. It was seven feet tall, had gold hair, gold eyes, and large golden wings. You'll notice that I call all of my angel teachers "it," for although they may manifest as celestial women or men, they are in essence neither male nor female, but both, and more.

Gabriel was my first angelic instructor, showing me how to open up to the angels and how to teach others to do that for themselves. The techniques I learned went into Ask Your Angels *and* Angel Answers. *Gabriel also taught me that however different our journeys have been, human souls and angels emerge from the same part of the heart of God, have a shared destiny, and need each other to fully realize themselves.*

*After its first vivid appearance, Gabriel gradually faded from sight,
but continued to speak to me as my other voices had, from deep within my
brain. After Gabriel, Raphael entered my life, and then several other angels. It wasn't until 1987 that I met my own guardian or companion angel,
Sargolais. And then in the summer of 1994 Gabriel began to speak to me
again. Its return to my life was a joyous time, a coming full circle.*

*The words you're about to read were dictated to me by Gabriel on
12 November 1994. Gabriel presents an overview of our place in the cosmos and also introduces the themes that are woven throughout the rest of
the book. Read these words slowly, preferably out loud. Feel them enter all
of your cells, and allow them to bathe you in angel visions. The word angel
means "messenger." Breathe these messages into your heart, your body,
your mind. They come from Gabriel as a gift to us in our journey to a new
era in human history.*

✳   ✳   ✳

Before there was time and space, God is. Before there were galaxies, stars, and planets turning, God is. Before there was life anywhere, unfolding and growing, God is.

What is, always has been, always will be. God is, and everything that is, is in God. And yet how can we say "in" of something
that is not about space, but is rather the Maker of space? And
how can we say "before" of something that is not about time,
but is rather the Maker of time? Words are intimations. They describe but cannot contain. God is. God was. God always will be.
Everything that is, is in, and of, and from, and with that which
we call God.

Galaxies, stars, and worlds. How wondrous is God's creation.
Some call it accident. We angels call it holy. Everything possible is
in God. Stars, worlds, life. For out of the beingness of God, everything arises and is of God too. Worlds, life, and people, in all their
different kinds, emerging, unfolding, filling what is with their own
God-created possibilities.

For God so loved possibilities that It created people, people on
millions of different worlds, people to dance and sing, people to
talk and laugh, people to love and share beauty. For God so loves
people that It has created them on billions of worlds, to know

what is and to celebrate that knowing, moment by moment, and day by day.

Seed and soul—together they rise up from the heart of God. People in thousands of dimensions, free and exploring creation—all of them emerge from the heart of God. How can it be otherwise than that our Maker has made a part of creation to mirror back to Itself what is? Infinite and unfolding, eternally creating, what is, is of the very nature of what was before it. And you, you human beings—you are of its very nature, too.

Boundless and yet woven into everything that is, God is never separate from what is. And when this universe was new, when conscious life was beginning to unfold in God's design, purposeful and free, that conscious life sang out to every star. And every star still carries within its own heart the joy of having been met and heard and felt and seen. Waiting to be known and met and loved, all of creation was waiting for people. And people are here.

Older worlds hungering for people birthed them, in millions of different ways. Beings that you would never recognize as people turned senses to the stars just as you do. And beings so like you in shape and thought—they too, on other worlds, turned hearts and minds toward all that is and rejoiced. And your world, too, a newer world, this world that you call Earth, wobbling on its axis, dancing its way around its star, this world that you call Earth—it wanted people, too. People to see its waters, its clouds, its trees, and its flowers. People to share joy and fill its heart with sound.

Many people. Many different kinds of people. Dancing on its tilted axis—that is what your planet wanted. Not one kind of people, but many. And slowly, over time, moving as a planet does, your Earth established its forms for people making. In the sea, and on land, your parent world created forms through time to unfold into possibility that which God had established in Its heart. People of the sea it birthed first, and then people of land. Wanting to weave into its patterns the essence of many other worlds, your Earth and the scattered other few like it put out a call to all dimensions, inviting the souls of hearty beings to journey here. Some came through space, others through time. Those in spirit dimensions—they did not have to travel at all to be here.

And so it was—over millions of years, weaving in souls from every part of this universe—that first sea and then land people emerged here, all of them holy, all of them unfolding from God's desire. And varied you are, both on sea and on land, varied and changing and beautiful, woven into your natures hundreds of other worlds and stars, woven into the matrix of your Earth-born bodies visions and memories and dreams from every part of the universe. For blue, white, brown, green swirling Earth so loves variety that it has woven into all its people souls from every part of God's universe.

The first sea people, together and in harmony, millions of years ago—they rose up from planet-tuned consciousness and sang to the stars. And the first land person—she a million years ago, Earth-body woven with souls from the stars, after a million years of spirit making ready, she your ancestress, she turned her heart and mind and eyes toward those stars and remembered them and loved them.

Djigi, the first human to be fully conscious in her body—she passed on her peopleness to her son, and he to all of his children. And now, a million years later, all of you are people, all of you are human. Land and sea people, each in your different ways, you are conscious, you are holy, you are God's possibility-loving children.

From the start, and slowly, from Djigi on down to you, gradually and over time, you have woven into your bodies more and more possibilities. The world was lush and rich when Djigi came. It was a garden, and so you remember it to have been. A garden, and yet who you are right now is far richer than anything Djigi ever knew.

A child on her hip, walking—that was how your history began. It could have begun in a million different ways as it did on a million different worlds. But that was how it happened here on Earth: that a woman knew God's universe, and then her son.

Spreading across the world, humans saw and knew and loved the Earth's beauty. Generation after generation, people changed and grew. And when the Earth passed through a distant place in its turning through the galaxy, and when the ice came, your ancestors did not die, but continued to grow. And that ice, which could have killed—it locked into your human bodies for all time the capacity to be whole and free. Spirit and matter together—that is what you are, and the coming of the ice evoked in you your highest possibilities, to dream, to make, to know.

Cold and then colder, in caves, around fires, your ancestors grew. Struggling and surviving, you have their courage alive in every cell of who you are. And when the ice began to recede, as your planet swung away from long winter domains, once again you began to move and change.

It was then, when the world opened itself to your courage, it was then that all over the world seers and elders saw the journey you could go on. And they gathered together to make maps of spirit. They gathered together bands of messenger folk, messenger tribes, to carry to every part of the globe their teaching words. The siblings Eshek and Miloak in what you call Europe, Matuae in the south of Africa, Chishak in central Asia, Kadik in India, whole villages of women and men in Australia, Hi Shua in China, Tenahila in the Americas—they and others all over your planet, they heard the words of your unfolding. They saw the journey you were about to go on. And like scouts who pack away provisions for an expedition, they stored up their words of wisdom for you to carry through the long and difficult journey into the world.

Before there was Abraham and Sarah, their ancestors Eshek and Miloak in what you call Spain were establishing the messenger tribes, to carry the food of spirit through your journey. Ten thousand years ago, they and the others like them in their different parts of the world gathered wisdom food together to last you through the journey.

Ten thousand years later, your journey nears its end. The provisions are nearly all consumed, just as they were meant to be. And soon you will all be arriving in your new home. This new home is not a place, for where in the world can you go that is new to you? And where in the stars could you go that would be more home than your Earth is to you? No, this new home you have struggled your way to is not a place but a way of being. For haven't all of your teachers—Moses, Mahavir, Jesus, Buddha, Muhammad—haven't all of the women and men who have been your teachers, known and forgotten, haven't they all told you of this place, this new garden?

The ice did not kill you. It forged you. What did not kill brought you to the place where you can kill. This world that did not kill you but clarified you has seen you arrive in the place where you could kill your world. And that—dear human people, that killing possibility—that is the mirror of your souls. Emerging from nothing but the heart of God, see this photograph of what is possible and remember who you are.

In what you have learned is your salvation. In all the pain and death and destruction, there lives the first and final hope. For what you are is possibility. And remembering that, you can become, all of you, the fulfillment of God's dream for you all. You can come home to the seed of who you are, now fully ready to unfold.

From tree to ground, from garden to ice, each stage in your journey has prepared you to become whole. Whole and holy. Fully human. All of you, snatching that marvel from the teeth of destruction. Now.

Come home. Be whole. In the garden of joy you will dwell. In the garden of love and dreams. Just as the Maker made everything, so too shall you in your garden make beauty and possibilities unfold. This is what you were created for. Not to be like angels, free to move from plane to plane. No, you were made to be people in form, in the world, embodied and holy and fully spirit at the same time. And this is what the journey of the last ten thousand years has taken you to. From the sealing of the ice, this journey after the ice withdrew has polished you and completed you. From death to death, you are alive.

Holy and beautiful you are, holy, embodied in form. The angels all celebrate you, who have emerged from God's heart by our sides and gone on this difficult and hearty journey.

Holy and wise, carrying the wisdom of the stars within you— stars, galaxies, and universes. All of that within you. For before there was time and space, the dream of you embodied souls was in God. And before there was life anywhere, the vision of you was alive in God. And here you are now, human and beautiful, wise, loving, holy. Embodied souls. In the midst of God's universe, ready to unfold the seed of possibility that was planted within you from long before you were born.

Wondrous and holy is God's universe. And from the beginning, the dream of people was a part of it. Billions of years of unfolding have led to the miracle of you. You as you are, miraculous and holy, embodied and alive. Who can see the farthest galaxy, who can peer into an atom. For whatever you see you touch, and whatever you touch is known. And whatever is known is fulfilled in God's creation. And it is for that that you were created—to touch, know, and love everything. Wondrous and holy, you are children of God.

Chapter 2

The Evolution of Human Life
on the Planet Earth

B efore I was communicating with angels, I was in dia-
logue with a number of other nonphysical beings that
I used to call guides and now think of as saints. I dis-
tinguish these saints, who have been human but are now
discarnate, from angels, who emerged from the same part
of the heart of God as we did but who have never incarnated, although they may take on human form.

The first saint to talk to me in my adult years appeared in 1976. I was taught by many saints over the
years, just as we have different teachers in elementary
school. The one I speak to most often now is named Arrasu, and I think of him as my college adviser. Except for
a brief return to physicality in the Renaissance, Arrasu
lived his last physical life at the end of the Ice Age. It is
his words that follow, which I transcribed in California
between 1993 and 1995. They are a fuller account of the
evolution of human life on our planet. As you read them,
allow your body-self to remember that this is our shared
history. Up until this time we have been unconscious of

so much of our past. To move to the next cycle in our history we need to be conscious of where we came from and where we have been.

﹡ ﹡ ﹡

I. Approximately five million years ago, Planet Earth, a lovely developing world in the Milky Way galaxy, put out a spirit call to every part of the universe: "Planet preparing for sentient life to evolve within the human frequency band looking for sentient rep resentatives of varied systems to initiate an experiment in multi-focused incarnation."

Beings from many different planetary systems and many different planes of reality answered this call, coming in wave after discarnate wave, to weave their many gifts into the energetic and physical structures of this planet.

When the first of these representatives arrived, they, in community with many angelic beings and with Earth itself, created a nonphysical collective of guiding spirits that can best be called a university. As newer representatives of other worlds arrived here, they were met by members of this Earth University and invited into its ranks.

The nonphysical members of the Earth University were involved in several different tasks. Some were information gatherers, others were dreaming their way into the planet's desires, and still others were working from nonphysical dimensions. Their task: to raise a certain species of physical beings to the point where they were capable of handling higher and more complex information frequencies.

There were many colleges within this university. These colleges were organized along the bands of the visible spectrum, whose different energies attracted different planetary representatives to them. So we may speak of the Red College, the Green College, the Blue College, and so forth.

For several million years the members of the university and its various colleges worked from the nonphysical dimensions to retune the genetic material of a prehuman primate species until it was ready to allow us to incarnate. In a sense, the process was like wiring a house. If the current in a house is too strong, it will burn out the wires. So you must install new wires if you want to "up" the current. After several million years of work, a physical form had been created that could carry the higher frequency of the souls of the members of the disembodied university. It was time to begin to incarnate.

The density of matter on Earth was not the same as it had been on most other worlds. Body structure and gender differences were major challenges, too. Also, some of us came from worlds where there was no suffering, no illness, no pain. And the particular neural capacities of the evolving species itself imposed further limitations. It wasn't always easy to adapt to these changes. Few of us in any of the colleges realized before incarnating how difficult it was going to be to live on Earth.

A planet that wobbles on its axis is always unstable. Poor, beautiful Earth had been struck by a wandering asteroid early in its history. This collision began the wobble, the rise and movement of continents, and impelled the soul of the planet to send out its beacon call. Only an unstable planet can put out such a call. Inviting human beings here was part of the planet's intention—not to stabilize its axis and the movements in its skin plates, but to create a conscious life-form that would complement its imbalances.

Life after incarnate lifetime the representatives of the university continued their work, as new souls emerged from the heart of God and entered Earth bodies for the first time. Death after death, we evolving beings went back to our colleges—to evaluate, to continue our studies, and to prepare for our reentry into physicality again.

Today, approximately two-thirds of all humanity began their cycles of incarnation here, and one-third of us are resident aliens who have lived on other worlds. Allow yourself some time to turn inward and ask yourself which group you belong to. All of us know in our hearts, and those around us know, too. If you were ever told by someone that you act like you come from another planet, and have never felt like you fit in here, it might be because you are from somewhere else. And if you relate to this glorious world like a tree growing up from it, never feeling separate from it, this may be your home world. Honor your history, honor your journey, for the representatives of each group carry precious gifts.

Each college in the university was responsible for different aspects of humanity's evolution and, from the nonphysical planes and from their increasing incarnations, altered the genetic structures of early human beings. The different races were developed by representatives of different planetary systems in the different colleges, with souls arriving here from more than a hundred different worlds. Art, music, and language, although woven through Earth bodies and reflecting Earth conditions, also carried strains of other worlds within them. And this process of weaving has continued up until this time.

On a soul level, it can be said that all incarnations—in fact, all of history—happens at the same time. But when you enter physicality, you must slow yourself down and move in linear space/time. And in addition to our physical lives, we were also exploring a host of possible and probable lives, on the Earth you call home and on several other parallel Earths. All of these realities are equally real, in different frequencies. So you may imagine how complex our training and our work have been.

Is it any wonder that it has taken us all this Earth time to get to the place we find ourselves in now—on the brink of full spiritual manifestation in physical bodies? And given the monumental task the university faced, is it any wonder that, as can happen with any experiment, the work we have done has not always been successful?

Often, once we were incarnate again, we forgot who we were and where we came from. The conditions of this planet, and the planet's wobble, interfered with the clarity of our remembrances. Sometimes our families and cultures recognized that there was something different about those of us from other worlds. In some places those differences were honored; in others, they were feared. Many of us were burned as witches, sent into exile, tortured, and/or turned into saints.

There is much we could regret. But we cannot complete our evaluation of human life on Earth yet. We are still in the midst of the grand experiment that the planet created for itself—to evolve a multifocused sentient incarnate life-form. We are all hovering on the edge of that eventuality. And now everything is changing. What was forgotten is being remembered again. And nothing is lost from all of human history. In our souls we carry the memories of every life we have lived here, of everything we learned, and of the reason we live here in the first place.

II. If you think that you come from another world or another dimension, now is the time to remember it. Open to your knowledge of how long you have been here, and to childhood memories and dreams of where you come from. Many resident aliens feel homesick, feel that they do not belong here. But deeper than this sense of disconnection can be found the vision and purpose that brought you here. Let yourself remember your home world. Let yourself feel the band of energy/information you brought here with you. Let yourself remember why you came here, for you are an ambassador of a different world, here to share your wisdom and perceptions in the Earth experiment.

If Earth is your home world, honor that in yourself. Honor the deep and pure connection you have to this planet, and use the power of that connection in your work. All of you have the capacity to transform life on this world when you honor Earth as the parent of your emergence. It is in harmony with your power as native Earthlings that those from other worlds must do their work, for Earth is home to you, and your love of Earth will be an inspiration for us all.

In between lives all Earthlings have participated in one of the six colleges in the Earth University. Some call this university the White Light Academy, for its full-spectrum energy. Now is the time to let yourself reach back into the color frequency of your own college within the greater university, so that you can feel and know your own area of expertise. In the simplest form, each college's work is aligned with energy of one of the primary colors of the visible spectrum, and each college's specialty concerns a particular area of human life.

The Red College:
survival needs; work with planet energies; shelter making; movement, physical expression, sports, and dance

The Orange College:
all forms of creativity; body needs and healing arts; fertility, work with animals and plants, food raising

The Yellow College:
organizations of all kinds, from government to business; expression of leadership in groups

The Green College:
intimacy; nurturance; childbirth and child rearing; education on all levels

The Blue College:
information accessing, gathering, and sharing; scientific exploration; communication on all levels; peacekeeping

The Purple College:
religious and spiritual connection; spiritual education; accessing and disseminating divine energy and wisdom

Although all of us have many different skills and carry the strands of different information bands, and have taken classes in all of the colleges, each one of us is a member of one primary college. Turn deeply into your soul. Explore your present and past history. Let yourself feel the inner/outer resonance of your primary frequency band, your color, your college.

When you have done this, reach out your consciousness to the teachers and advisers who have been supporting you since your arrival or emergence on this world—and begin to make conscious contact with these beings who are your own teachers, if you have not done so already. Generally, all university members have one main adviser from the human frequency band, who may also come from your home world, and one from the angelic band. Become conscious of both of your advisers, and begin communicating with them on an ongoing basis, as partners in the next phase of our transformational work. Often, close friends and partners from the same home world and college do not incarnate at the same time. Be aware of the profound support and guidance that can come from these now-discarnate friends also, whom you have supported when they were incarnate and you were between lives.

All the work that you have been doing in the world is vital and necessary, but until you become conscious of your university connections, your work will move in endless circles, neither deepening itself into the planet nor rising to the stars. It will not be soul fulfilling. And this lack of satisfaction will be reflected in your lives. Frequently, embodied university members overwork to compensate for this sense of disconnection. When you are connected and doing your work, you will not feel tired, and you will have sufficient time to rest, play, and cultivate new skills and pleasures, and also time enough to enjoy the company of others.

Many incarnate members of the university have spent time exploring past lives. This work is vital for some, but not for everyone. You are living in a critical period. You have two more years to complete your personal work, and this includes past-life exploration. After this two-year period is over, there will be seventeen years in which the focus, physical and energetic, will be primarily directed toward healing Earth, and not toward your own or even other people's personal healings.

Given this mandate, which is coming to us from the planet itself, it is far more important to reconnect on a soul level with the knowledge we brought with us and have gathered while being here than it is to remember all of our incarnational history. However, knowing that all of us were approaching this critical era, in your three previous incarnations you worked to activate the wisdom you gathered in all of your earlier incarnations. All of this information was encoded in those last three lives, and if you remember them you will become conscious of everything you need to know about your full Earth history, incarnate and discarnate.

Ultimately, however, all of your soul history is contained in this, your present life. There are five basic areas in your current lives that reflect your multidimensionality. Hold as your goal that all five of them can be functioning fully, and all five of them can be in balance. In reading through this list, use it as a diagnostic for the particular personal work that you can be doing in this time of transformation.

1. If your work lives are not fulfilling, if you do not feel at this time that you are doing your life's work, then you are ready to

become conscious of your primary purpose in incarnating in this period. The form of work you do is not important. Do not judge work by social standards, but by your capacity to be present in what you do, and by your ability to resonate clear and loving information, from whatever is your college's area of expertise. For example, if you came in to share healing energy, you may in fact find it limiting to be a doctor, acupuncturist, massage therapist, herbalist, or chiropractor. Some of the finest healers in Earth history have been hairdressers and waitresses, who do their work for humankind invisibly.

2. If your intimate relationships are not satisfying, if you are not loved and loving in your life, then you are probably disconnected from the ultimate source of love that permeates the universe. Remember, love can come to us from a stone, a tree, a beloved dog, a flower, a cloud, a star, and not just from a spouse, a child, or any kind of human lover. Love has far more forms than any of us on this planet know. The journey toward being able to express and experience all of them is part of our purpose in being here. So remember—every lover, be it tree, dog, or human, is but a finger pointing to the Ultimate Beloved.

3. If your relationships with your biological families are not healed, then you may be out of touch with the varying aspects of your own past selves. In this lifetime, each of you has very carefully chosen family members whose gifts, and also whose flaws and limitations, will mirror back to you aspects of your own greater self. So if you have not come to accept as they are all the members of your extended families, you may still have work to do in accepting your own nature and owning all of who you have been yourself. Even abusive parents mirror back something from the past. You may not be able to forgive them, but allow yourself to see them in a larger frame, as evolving beings struggling to master physicality and not succeeding at it, which is something that has happened to all of us.

4. If your relationships with friends are limited or not satisfying, if you are not communicating clearly with the people you live

and work with, then you may not have owned the complexity of who you are and may be disconnected from the varying bands of information you need to work with in your dealings with other college members. For in every stage of this life you have chosen friends to reflect your multidimensionality. If you do not have some contact with people from each phase of your life, and if you are not continuing to make new friends who come from different colleges and have increasingly different interests, then this is an area you have the opportunity to heal in your present life.

5. Finally, your relationship to the Planet Earth itself needs to be whole and loving. If you still feel alien from your body, from other life-forms, and from this world itself, you are still living in separation from our ultimate and ever-present home in All That Is. Self-massage and self-nurturing, spending time in nature, being involved in healing the planet—these will help to balance any polarization you may still feel between spirit and matter, mind and body. Doing this will ground everything you brought with you from other lives and other worlds into your present body and into the greater body of our beautiful Earth.

III. Living on Earth is a perpetual gift and an ongoing challenge. The simplest gift is the basic ability to incarnate. For, however damaged, Earth is still a rich and vibrant and beautiful world, teeming with life, adventure, and sensual delight. Let yourself taste all of Earth's free gifts: sunrise, flowers, the wonder of a flock of birds in flight, the kinship of others, and the joy of friendship, which is the greatest gift of all. In opening your life to others, you embrace all of creation. For on this world there are people from every part of this universe—and from several others, too. In communing with them, you connect with all the universe.

The greatest challenge of all on this world has been learning to handle the diversity, the richness, the violence, and the depth of its emotions. Few other worlds have so varied and complex an emotional palette as this world has; for few other worlds have emotional strands woven in from so many different worlds. Incarnate university members often suffer emotional pain that they attempt to block out, primarily through the use of drugs, denial, and self-deflecting care of others. Explore these aspects of your own self and use them to heal your own bodies. And now is the time for us to remember the wisdom we brought here as immortal souls, the wounds we have suffered here, and the ultimate reason we chose to be born here, which is to express our innate love of physicality.

A child learns to respect the power of fire the first time it burns its hand. An incarnate soul may need a thousand lifetimes to master the fire of Earth emotions. And it may take a species a million years to learn to master the raging complexities of human existence on a complex world like Earth. But every single incarnation is a gift, however painful. And now that a million years of our incarnational history have passed, we stand at the brink of global transformation. Down through the ages, instructors from the Earth University have been incarnating in every culture, in every time, to show by their lives what it means to be fully human, fully incarnate. And now, for the first time in our history, we live in a world where all of humanity is ready to be fully incarnate, however unlikely that appears when we listen to the news. But the time is at hand, and all that is required of us now, as members of the colleges of the University of Earth, is that we own all of our love and wisdom, and beam it out to all the world.

Just as our beautiful planet evolved a sentient life-form that lives on the Earth, it also created for itself a sentient life-form that lives in the waters. The sea people—dolphins and whales—given their different history, reached a place of conscious awareness in their own frequency bands millions of years before we did. In a sense it might be said that they are the indigenous sentient beings of this world, and we humans are the newcomers. They too, however, have their own off-world connections, for the band of sentience they embody has manifested itself on numerous other worlds. We humans cannot enter into the next cycle of our history without making conscious contact with the cetaceans. Let it be remembered that cetaceans and humans are the two hemispheres of this planet's sentient neural net, and when they work together, the work of the planet itself is facilitated.

Open yourself now to the people of the sea. Feel the presence of their wise and very different consciousness. Spend time by the waters if you can, but know that simply by reaching out to the energy of the cetaceans you can open yourself to their wisdom. Each of the human colleges has its own connections with different families of sea people. Reach out through your own college and discover the particular cetacean beings you are connected to, and your own embodied work will deepen and flow out into the world. Alone, neither of this planet's peoples can do the work of embodiment the planet created us for. Together, in harmony with each other's differences, we can.

As the planet was moving toward physical sentience, it created backup systems should either experiment fail. The backup for the cetaceans was the elephants. Had sentience not taken hold in the cetaceans, the planet would have directed the ancestors of the present-day elephants to carry that band of consciousness. And on land, had the experiment with primates failed, the bear people would have carried on the work of evolution. To this day, because of their potential backup work, the elephants and the bears are threshold guardians, doorways to possibility. They stand as bridges to the animal realms, and when you reach out to them you further connect yourself to the planet, to the multitude of other beings who live here, and to the great and glorious work the planet has chosen for itself.

So together with the angels, with the ancestors from all of their different worlds, in alignment with the others of your Earth college, and with the support of the cetaceans, the elephants, and the bears, you can carry on your soul work in this moment—alive, and whole, and purposeful.

IV. Earth is a difficult and beautiful world. Once members of the university began to incarnate, they were met with even more difficult conditions. Thus, over time, one of the major functions of the university has been the after-death rehabilitation of its members.

Just as a room can be filled with broadcast waves from multiple stations, with none of them interfering with each other, so too the various frequencies, facilities, classrooms, and healing rooms of the university all coexist. Depending on a given person's needs at death, these different energetic reality zones may appear as, variously, Jewish heaven, Buddhist hell, Catholic limbo, an existentialist's No Exit, or any of an infinitely expansive number of independently created realms. These realms are created in harmony with the soul entity of a given individual, and in alignment with its different guides and angels.

In your embodied terms, entities come back to these rehab zones between lives. But the time between lives is fluid, expansive, and all of it is interconnected. Depending on an entity's personal awareness, it may or may not realize that it is in rehab. Or rather, it may or may not realize that the "reality" it finds itself in is a created one, designed to heal and educate.

During its stay in a university rehab unit, the various aspects of the self will be healed, taught, guided. This is a time for reflection on a completed incarnation, and, as entities become more aware, this is a time to plan out succeeding incarnations. This is also a time for entities to work out agreements with each other. Families will gather here, together, to plan out further group adventures. Soul tribes will also meet, and lay strands of information that will connect them later. This is not unlike groups of fashion designers who gather together to decide on the following year's colors, even if they seem to be rivals once their new garments appear.

There is much agreement and disagreement among members of soul tribes, and among members of the different colleges in the university. Disagreement shapes reality just as much as agreement does. And incarnate life is an opportunity to test different theories of physical growth and learning.

There is no reason to suppose that we who teach in the university are absolute masters of incarnating. Although we come from different worlds, we ourselves are still learning. And very often a master in one incarnation returns to rehab and becomes the student of a former incarnate student. Very often soul-tribe entities take turns incarnating, the discarnate ones becoming each other's backup teams.

Many of the techniques for physical healing that you are beginning to practice on Earth are things that you have learned here.

The ancient mystery schools of your historical past all tapped into the disembodied university, but none of them could bring through consciously as much information as you are able to assimilate in your bodies at this time. The soul weight of the body is larger now, in greater numbers of individuals, than it has ever been before at any time in human incarnate history on this world.

Out of your physical form, back in the university, it is easier to reconnect with your purpose in coming here. The challenge has always been to integrate that information when you were back in a physical body. There is no ultimate sin, no essential flaw, connected to all the ways in which you think you have failed in this and other lives. They are the only—we repeat, *only*—way that you could have learned what you needed to learn, on this particular world. On other worlds, it *is* easier. But you came *here*. You came here for the challenge. Even at your weakest, remember that you came here because you are hardy, tough, and seeking soul adventure.

In rehab you get to be you in your wholeness and perfection. In rehab you can taste soul and God clearly again. But the purpose of your existence, of all of our existences, is to incarnate, to weave a certain frequency of consciousness into physicality. It was for that that the Creator created you. And if you forget that in a given incarnation, in rehab you will surely remember it. True, you may have to cycle through different soul-directed "rehabilitative hells." But eventually you will feel your way out of ice or fire. And when you do that, and come back consciously to the university, you will be making ready to come back to Earth. For it is only when we have fully mastered physicality that we can consider going on.

Please know and remember that there is no such thing as eternal damnation. The courses of study in the university are not eternal, either. You may forget what you learned when you come back to Earth, but you forget only consciously. The information you have absorbed is still carried in all of your cells, physical and nonphysical. Up until the present the human body and the human brain have not been ready to consciously handle this kind of information. But the work we have been doing in form has changed this. Your brains are awakening to their full potential, and more and more of you are "remembering" things that only a few of us in every generation could remember before. And together as a family we are ready to create on Earth the kind of embodied heaven that we have been dreaming of and working toward for all these million years. For the soul is never separate from God, from cosmic wisdom. And now, in this time, no matter how unlikely it might seem if you read the morning paper or listen to the horrors in the news each night—now, for the first time in all of human history, the human body itself has evolved to the place where it too will know that it is never separate from God.

Chapter 3

THE ORIGINS OF CIVILIZATION ON THE PLANET EARTH

*T*he material in this section also comes from my Earth University adviser, Arrasu. Having read the previous section, you may be opening to conscious connection with your own adviser. As you move in the world, be conscious of the people in your life. Ask yourself which of your friends and family come from the same college as you do. Often we meet such old-time friends and think that the depth of connection is about romantic love, and enter into relationships that do not honor our true connection.

Many of our religions have told us that physicality is a punishment, that being in a physical body is a sign that we have fallen from divine grace, forgotten our true natures. But what the angels and saints tell me is that God created us to become physical, and that mastering physicality is the goal of our existence. By this I do not mean just being in a body, but being physical together so that we can create a world of joy and love and truth and beauty. Just as a tree must have strong and healthy roots to live, we need to know our own roots to thrive. In this *section you will find the story of the very first civilization on the planet, the first attempt by our ancestors to embody consciously.*

✳ ✳ ✳

Five million years ago this planet put out a call to incarnate sentients of a certain kind who were living on other worlds. The call expressed this planet's desire to create for itself a novel form of sentience, one that wove together representatives from many different worlds. Earth had already created physical vehicles for the form of sentience that is carried by the dolphins and whales. But it wanted a second variety, one that would complement theirs. And from every part of this universe, beings who had heard Earth's call began to arrive here, disembodied, to participate in Earth's experiment.

After three million years of attention from the nonphysical dimensions, working with an evolving protosentient primate species, a physical life-form had evolved that was capable of handling basic human frequencies.

This work was collective, and involved numerous representatives from seven different planetary systems, plus lesser numbers from numerous other worlds—all of them working in collaboration with devas, angels, and the planet itself. Slowly, over the next two million years, different entities began to incarnate in these newly evolved forms, as waves of other entities continued to arrive here. Together, they worked to tune their chosen physical bodies from within, altering their genetic structures and raising their vibrational capacities.

At the same time, in nonphysical planes, entities were working to create Earth cultures that would weave together the patterns of sentience brought here from other worlds. Numerous nonphysical experiments were held, to test out different cultures and learn from them. These experiments occurred in alternate dimensions, like vast collective dreams. The entities who participated in these collective cultures worked together to make ready our species for full incarnation.

These experiments are known by different names—Atlantis, Lemuria, Mu. Each of them allowed us to explore a different territory in consciousness, and each one furthered the evolution of our species. Eventually, we created an experiment in Kandayata, a "lost continent" in the nonphysical dimensions coexistent with the Indian Ocean, that was successful in all areas, individual and collective. Life in Kandayata was peaceful and richly creative, without power struggles and with balance between genders and among all its blue-skinned inhabitants. Technology was created that was harmonious with the planet and supportive of human needs. At that point it was clear that our souls and the physical vehicles that had been created for them to incarnate in were ready for a massive inflow of disembodied souls.

This happened approximately one hundred thousand years ago. Since that time, more and more of us have been incarnating here, participating in the next level of our evolutionary experiment—the creation of what we call civilization.

True, there have always been challenges here. But our collective strength was great, and we knew that, just as birds are not born flying but must at some point leap out from their nests, so we were ready and in fact needed to leap out from our nonphysical civilizations into the fertile and rich world of full physicality. Many have seen this stepping into matter as a fall from grace, guided by fallen angels. But we in the university see it and remember it as a time of bravery and clarity instead.

Many of us look to Atlantis and Lemuria for the origins of civilization. Others, looking back at our history, think that the emergence of civilization began several thousand years ago in Egypt and Mesopotamia, in India and China. We forget that even those civilizations had roots. We ignore what the brilliant and sophisticated art of the so-called cavemen tells us about human consciousness from the middle of the last Ice Age. And we know nothing at all of the very first civilization to emerge on our physical planet, on the verdant plains of Africa in what is now the Sahara, in the time before the ice made its last major descent.

This prime civilization established patterns in human consciousness that have shaped and guided all subsequent cultures on this planet. The name of this long-forgotten civilization was Ushtu.

The history of Ushtu is lost to our conscious minds, but it is carried in the memory banks of all of us, encoded deep within our genetic structures. Memories of Ushtu also reside within the collective unconscious of our species, and within the morphogenetic field—that web of energy and information that encircles our planet, that all of us are plugged into. With a warm climate, and with lush vegetation that provided food in abundance, Ushtu was the Garden of Eden, the Paradise, the Golden Age that so many different cultures remember in their myths.

Rituals and belief structures that are shared by all humanity were encoded into us by our ancestors in the time when Ushtu flourished, starting approximately ninety thousand years ago and continuing until the ice sheets began to advance and climate shifts initiated migratory changes that sent our ancestors to every part of this planet.

A stable society whose culture flourished for thousands of years, Ushtu was rich in music, dance, stories, and portable art. Everything made by our forebears was drawn upon, painted, carved, and made beautiful. Little of this civilization remains, although recently, from above the Earth's surface, evidence of the ancient rivers of the Sahara have been found, and in time artifacts of the people who once lived there may also be discovered.

At its height, many thousands of people lived in or in proximity to the main centers of life in Ushtu, both in northern and in southern Africa. There were networks of settlements that sprang up around the many rivers, with people both walking and rafting from village to village. Peace reigned in Ushtu. There were no hostilities. Each village was controlled by a council of elders, all female, who appointed the male chiefs and ceremonial leaders. This balance of power, and a matrilineal kinship system, lasted all through the existence of this forgotten civilization.

Once basic patterns of group cooperation were established in Ushtu, many of the representatives from other worlds began incarnating. Their purpose was to teach those souls who were newly emerging into incarnation on this planet. The rudiments of art, agriculture, and spirituality were shared with the people of Ushtu, taught by specialists from different worlds, all of whom had participated in the creation of nonphysical cultures prior to this time.

Through song, dance, and storytelling, information was passed on, from elders to the people, down through the generations. The origins of shamanism date back to Ushtu and its elders. The earliest buildings and monuments aligned with the planet's energy flows can also be traced back to Ushtu. A common spoken language linked all of its residents. And to this day, all human beings organize thoughts and actions in patterns that evolved on the physical plane among our forebears in Africa.

Before Ushtu, our ancestors were tool-making, upright primates who possessed the ability to speak and the basics of cooperation. They stood on the edge of animal consciousness, not yet sentient. But ever since Ushtu, we have been sentient human beings.

It is easy to look at human history and see it as a trail of tears. Our experiment, like all such attempts in any part of the universe, has been long and difficult. But if you look at it from the discarnate plane, you will see a slow and gradual evolution of sentience being pioneered on this planet by hosts of immortal, reincarnating souls.

It isn't easy to become human, especially when so many different strands are being woven in, and given a world as physically unstable as our home. On most other worlds, you will not find this rich mixture of elements, or the physical challenges set up by the planet. Earth's experiment is a rare one, and because of that, we have been observed by many different races, both physical and nonphysical, some of them nurturant and others power-based. But the heart of this planet pulses with generosity. Energies antithetical to the planet's deep nature can live on the surface, but cannot sink deep roots here. And because of that, the experiment we began at Ushtu not so very long ago is about to reach fruition.

From a cluster of little grass-hut villages built in circles, all of them about a day's walk from each other, we have created the beginning of a global culture. Though wars still rage on different parts of this planet, though people still go to bed hungry (if they have a bed at all), many of us can walk into music stores and buy circular discs encoded with music from every part of this planet, or pick up a telephone and speak instantly to someone on the other side of the world.

In the past, in every culture that emerged here, there were individuals who could carry full human sentience in the fibers of their bodies. Many of these great teachers are still known, but most of them have been forgotten by history. Over time, more and more individuals have been appearing who could hold these frequencies. And we are moving toward a time when everyone here will be fully sentient, when everyone here will be wise and loving and whole. When that happens, the emerging global culture we are creating will flower and grow strong.

Together we are standing on a threshold, a twenty-year-long threshold of possibility. Together, we heirs of ancient Ushtu can transform our warring world into one of rich, creative peace. There is enough food to feed everyone, and enough material resources to house and clothe everyone. Our physical needs are varied enough to provide everyone with pleasurable and purposeful employment. With the right shifts, our world can be structured to evolve in harmony with the planet and with all the varied life-forms that live here, both physical and nonphysical.

The promise of this kind of civilization was imprinted on our genes in the heart of Africa. We have only to step inside ourselves to find it. In the dark of night, looking up at the stars, we can remember that many of our ancestors came from distant places, came here to participate in a novel adventure in consciousness. To the sound of drums, to the rhythmic chant of our own voices, to simple flutes and the stamping feet of dancers, we can connect with the primal dreams of those ancestors, many of whom were our own past selves in other times and places.

The promise of incarnate life woven into our ancestors' genetic material in Ushtu has been taught in every culture on this planet: "Love one another, help one another, share equally the rich and nurturing resources of this planet." These basic truths are global, encoded in all of our bodies. We know that life could be better than it is, we can all dream of a better world, because of Ushtu. Without it, we would have no dreams.

Feel the information that you carry within you from Ushtu. Remember a place and time when copper-orange-skinned people, of a color that no longer appears here, created the first civilization on this planet. Feel the dreams you carry within you from that time. Know that your history is a rich one, that you carry the marvel of Ushtu inside. Know too that you are alive now to participate in the unfolding of a process that began so very long ago, when the Sahara was still lush and beautiful, and our species was still young.

When our astronauts looked back on Earth for the first time, they saw a shimmering blue pearl below their tiny craft. A single photograph of our planet taken from space now appears on posters and cards and book covers. This picture has become a calling card of our shared destiny. A circular image. White clouds swirling up from the bottom. Blue ocean surrounding a brownish-green landmass near the top of the picture. It is Africa that you are looking down upon. Your eye follows the photographer's eye— right over the once-fertile plain that gave birth to ancient Ushtu.

Five million years ago this beautiful blue-green planet decided to host an experiment in the evolution of sentience. Two million years ago a species evolved that was capable of fulfilling the planet's desire. One hundred thousand years ago in Africa, that species reached a level of rich intensity and sent its members out to every part of the globe. Today, together, in our time, we can initiate the global shifts in consciousness that will announce to the universe that that experiment was a success.

It was in Ushtu that we began the journey that brings us to this time. Ushtu is the primal paradise spoken of in myths from every part of this planet. It colors all our dreams. Ushtu was the childhood of our species. It was our Eden. And as we allow ourselves to remember it, the future world that we are creating will emerge from the roots of that long-forgotten time.

Chapter 4

THE FIRST COVENANT

 Knowing the roots of global civilization, we can now explore the earliest roots of the civilization that has spread across the globe, the culture of the West. Also known as the Judeo-Christian-Islamic civilization, this culture has dominated the planet in recent centuries, and knowing about its roots will give us insight into ways that we can transform it from within.

Although it has rich roots in many different places, from ancient Egypt to Greece, from Persia to the world of the Celts, Western civilization is grounded today in the scriptures of the ancient Hebrews. Our morality and culture have been shaped by those documents whether we are religious fundamentalists or secular humanists. Like the air we breathe, this grounding is invisible and ever-present.

What are the roots of that culture? According to Arrasu, our spiritual history as Western people is even older than we think, older than our scriptures, going back even further in time than we can imagine. Knowing our roots can empower us to grow in wisdom and strength as we create a new global civilization. In the words that follow you can explore these roots for yourself.

✳   ✳   ✳

What you call Western civilization did not begin in Mesopotamia or in the Nile Valley. The origins of this vast and diverse culture can actually be traced back to the western Mediterranean, to the coast of what is now called Spain. Far older than you imagine, Western civilization goes back to the days of the end of the last Ice Age, to the world that followed after Ushtu.

As the ice began to recede, patterns of culture that had served humanity for thousands and thousands of years were becoming obsolete. Ways of living in and out of the world, in trance, out of body, were being replaced by a far more physically focused exploration of life. This was appropriate and inevitable in the evolution of a sentient species. From the roots of a culture the trunk and branches grow. So, rooted in a deep connection to the earth and to the spirit realms, your people began to step away and explore the world itself. Ten thousand years later, you find yourselves at the end of the cycle of history that began then. You find yourselves at a time in your history when the fruits of your struggle are ready to be eaten.

The end of a cycle always calls forth the energy of its beginning. So in speaking to you now of that time, we also speak to you of the history of your own people. For the history of the Hebrews does not date back to the city of Ur in Mesopotamia, nor does it go back to the discovery of a single God by a man named Abraham. Your history is far older than that. It, too, dates back to the origins of Western civilization.

As the ice withdrew, as people were able to spread about and explore the globe again, the ties that bound all the world's people together were being pulled apart. But certain truths that were rooted in the collective psyche still needed to be remembered. So at that time, in many different parts of the globe, groups of people, not all of them biological kin, chose to come together and work together as messenger tribes. Not only did these people bond together on a day-to-day level, and on an energetic level, but they bonded together in the collective information banks of the species itself. This bonding was so powerful that these people were able to imprint their genetic material and pass on their connection and their purpose to their physical heirs.

The work of the messenger tribes was expressed in space and time. As the world grew warmer, as people began to spread out, the work of the messenger tribes was to carry information from place to place, to keep a species connected in the physical world as it had once been connected on the spiritual plane. In addition to being news bearers, these tribes were also carriers of the ancient wisdom that had linked all of humanity together.

These messenger tribes did not serve themselves. They served the species, and were chosen by the species. There were messenger tribes all over the globe. In the East, where the species' collective decision to explore physicality was not as directed as it was in the West, the function of the messenger tribes was not so essential. There, over time, the people as a whole remembered more of the root wisdom, and eventually most of their messenger tribes were absorbed back into other tribes and peoples. However, the Gypsies still carry their messenger history from Asia, and the inhabitants of Australia are to this day a tribe of messenger people, self-contained and carrying wisdom for all of humanity.

In the West, where the species collectively chose to explore physicality to the fullest, the need for messenger tribes was stronger. The original covenant between Spirit and the messenger peoples, the original covenant made by the ancestors of the Hebrews, did not happen at Mount Sinai, or between God and Abraham. It happened on the eastern coast of Spain, in a large encampment called Inathid, now buried under the sea. It was in Inathid that the very first stone circle, the ancestor of all the Stonehenges, was built. And it was in Inathid, as the ice withdrew, that a gathering of people—deeply in trance, deeply in connection with Spirit and the collective will of humanity, remembering the journey that began at Ushtu—chose for themselves, and for anyone who incarnated into the bodies of their descendants, the task of being messenger people for their civilization.

From Spain, civilization as you know it spread out across the Mediterranean, into parts of Europe, Asia, Africa. As diverse as the peoples of these continents are, they were once linked by the constant wanderings of the messenger tribes. Wisdom and history were carried and remembered by this people. But civilization grew, and the old wandering ways of life were replaced by a life of cities and countries and borders. The work of the messenger tribes was ignored, forgotten. Each different culture was inventing its own roots, its own history—separate from the shared collective history the messenger tribes recalled. In time, many of the messenger people married out of their tribes and forgot the ancient language that they all had shared, which was related to the language of the Basque people.

It seems as if the story of the Hebrews began with Abraham. And Abraham was a real person, even if many of the stories told about him are only that. But this Abraham was a member of a messenger tribe—and he knew it. He remembered his work, but he did not work alone. There were in his vicinity twenty-seven people who were still committed to the work their ancestors had passed on to them. They remembered the covenant at Inathid, and the long cycles of information that mothers passed on to their sons and fathers passed on to their daughters. Seeing the world around them, the wars and killings that were more destructive than the ice, they gathered together and swore a contract, with God and with each other, to carry on the messenger work, no matter how difficult, unwanted, or superfluous it seemed.

Although this too has been forgotten by history, it was under the leadership of Sarah, whose name means "princess," and to whom Abraham was married, that these people set out from Mesopotamia to connect with the only other band of messenger people they knew still existed. This other band lived in Canaan, under the guidance of a man called Melchizedek. The coming together of these two bands was joyous. Each brought the other a renewed sense of history and purpose. And from that reunion of clans, the beginning of the history of this people as you have known it was born, and the adoption of a new language that you call Hebrew, by the clan from Mesopotamia.

The Western Scriptures—Hebrew, Greek, and Arabic—are largely the work of the descendants of the messengers. Just as Sarah and Abraham and Moses and Jesus were genetic heirs to the people from Inathid, so too was Muhammad. Each in their own way carried on another part of the collective spiritual history of

Western civilization. Not everything in these scriptures is true, but the kernel of truth in each of them is a vital part of your lives.

Much of what you read now was written down hundreds and thousands of years after it was spoken. The scribes and prophets who recorded it had lost the purity of memory their ancestors had, and much of the material was also edited later on to conform to the cultural expectations of different places and times. So, for example, Sarah's story is obscured, given over to her husband by later historians. The story of Adam and Eve and the Garden of Eden was edited too, a simplified version of a much longer saga that included references to Inathid and the land of the West. Indeed, the true history of the messenger tribes was forgotten completely—on a conscious level. Their journeys around the Great Sea, the Mediterranean, and how they finally came to Mesopotamia, were all forgotten. But when the descendants of these people came back to Spain thousands of years later, an unconscious part of them remembered their earliest history, and it flourished in the kabbalistic wisdom preserved there. And they participated in a rich and diverse culture that is still called the Golden Age in Spain, and represents a high point in your civilization, for Jews, Christians, and Muslims alike—each of these another branch on the tree of Western civilization.

The history of the Jews, their wanderings, struggle, purpose, all go back to the covenant made at Inathid. The founders of the Christian and Islamic traditions were also related to the messenger tribes. History has forgotten the woman Devorah, elder sister of Jesus' grandmother Hannah and his primary teacher, who passed on to him the wisdom of the messengers. As it has forgotten the schools started by his students Lazarus, Mary of Magdala, Martha, and John the beloved, the last of whose lineage continued in secret until this century, when the final direct follower died in France, and whose students included da Vinci, Galileo, and Copernicus. And so too history has almost entirely forgotten Muhammad's teacher Khidr, his wife's uncle, another bearer of messenger wisdom. Of him only the most shadowy stories remain, enshrined by the great Sufi teachers, who carried most purely the simple messages of the past.

The covenant of the messenger tribes is wired into your genetic structures. All Jews carry this history, chosen by their souls before birth; it fulfills an aspect of their own essential nature, as seekers, wanderers, rememberers. And yes, there has been pain and suffering. But through the suffering there has been joy and, beneath the joy, a continual sense of purpose for all of human civilization.

Not Jews alone but all of you carry in your genetic structures the imprinting of the first messenger tribe. For the messenger peoples have intermarried all across the planet, and you all carry their work inside you, even though a conscious memory of it has been lost. So at the end of an era that began as the ice withdrew, it is time for the messages carried by the messenger tribes to come to the surface and be remembered again. And what is the heart of these messages? That we all come from God, and are never separate from It. The creation story is a reminder of that, as was the message of Jesus, who taught that *everyone is a child of God,* that *we are all one people.* The tale of Adam and Eve is a reminder of that. The one who dictates these words belonged to the messenger tribe, was present at Inathid, and still carries that covenant with him. The one who takes his dictation is also an heir to the messenger tribe. And what of the ones who read these words now? What do you remember? What do you remember that belongs to everyone?

Chapter 5

A Gathering of Unknown Saints

Enlightenment *is one name for the attainment of a certain level of embodied consciousness, when a soul fully manifests in the physical world. In the past, only a few individuals in each generation realized this state. But at this time in our history, we have all lived many lives, learned and grown in many different ways, and have access to the work of the messenger tribes and of masters from every age and from every part of the planet, and now the realization of embodied sentience is possible for every one of us.*

When we think about the enlightened teachers of the past, we may remember only Christ or Buddha. But there are many Christs and many Buddhas. Some are still revered in distant corners of the world, some have been forgotten through time, while the stories of others have been deliberately obscured by those who came after them but did not embrace their visions of wholeness.

The vow of awakened teachers—to continue to share their wisdom until all sentient beings are enlightened— can be fulfilled by their coming back to Earth again and again, or it can be satisfied from the discarnate plane. The saints presented in this section are all beings who have chosen to fulfill that vow as nonphysical teachers, as instructors and advisers in the Earth University.

The information on these forgotten saints was given to me in the summer of 1982 by Tayarti, another discarnate teacher of mine from the end of the last Ice Age. Over the years I have reached out to all of the saints in this section, felt the comfort of their presence, and put down on paper some of what they taught me.

Although the form of their teachings varies, there is one concept that all of these unknown sages agree upon: that our bodies are holy, that the Earth is holy, and that the way for us to transform life on this planet is to remember this and to live from this remembering.

Enlightenment isn't something that we have to achieve. It is something that exists within us all the time. As you read these words, feel the wisdom and holiness of your body and of the world. Reach out to these unknown saints, and let their wisdom mirror back to you your innate light, your own clear inner guidance. Feel it, own it, and move in the world in such a way that you mirror it back to everyone you see, to the trees, the animals, the sky, the water, the air, and Planet Earth itself.

✸ ✸ ✸

AKKUB lived in the twelfth century of this era, among the ancestors of the Ashanti people. When her husband and children were killed in a skirmish with a neighboring tribe, Akkub went into hiding for three years, feeling the grief of Africa in her soul, past and future grief, as a woman and mother alone.

In a hut she built for herself, living off food she gathered for herself, Akkub spent her time alone, praying and meditating. At first she prayed about anger, injustice, and pain. But none of the ancestors or tribal gods could answer her. So she turned to a greater source, and vowed not to leave her retreat till an answer came to her or till she died, whichever came first. She came to see herself in a game too vast for rules. And in her waiting, as she unfolded herself, enlightenment came to her, swiftly and cleanly as a bird in flight.

From her experience came her teaching. And the simplicity of her words was her strength. For her message was this: that life is a flow, and we can be in it or out of it. It is better to be in it, so at every moment we must be aware of the ebbs and currents. We must be listening and watching at all times, as if for the wind. Therefore we regulate our lives. Not to stifle, but to make simplicity and order, so as not to be distracted from listening.

Akkub is one of the greatest of the forgotten world sages. She taught in her lifetime, in the years after her enlightenment, wandering from village to village. Only the warring of her descendants and the destruction and chaos of the European invasions put a stop to the memory of her work. Nonetheless, as always since her death, Akkub has remained in the spirit world, helpful, present to all who call on her in love for greater understanding.

Some Words of Akkub

This I have found. . . . Spirit there is which pervades everything, like light in a room. Which cannot be touched. Like water in a pool, inseparable from the world for the creatures of that water. Yet this Spirit is that from which all the other things—the light, the water—are derived. I say derived, but not in the way that flour is derived from grain. The world is derived from this Spirit as is dance derived from the dancer, one and the same, an expression of the One and not a change in it.

I saw a child, and it was playing in the lap of its mother. And I saw the look of purity in its eye. And I knew that it might leave that look forever to live in the world. And I wanted to say to that child, "Child, hold fast to that slow tilting look in your eye." But the child could not understand speech.

Once I saw myself as like that child, but I could not go back to that feeling. And I asked myself, "Akkub, maybe, perhaps, the way of that child is the right way." But later I said to myself that if that were the right way, no one should be unhappy.

This I have found. . . . There is a way of being in the world that makes for ease. The old teachers talk of this, and they say that the way is of obedience to the gods. But I have found that there is another way, a simple way. And this I would like to tell to you. For I have suffered much to find it on my own. And now I give it away, as a tree gives up its blossoms to the hair of a lover.

This I have found. . . . On nights when I sat alone in my darkness. Listening to the wind shimmering through the trees around my hut. That there is a stillness in the world, and a stillness inside me. And the two different stillnesses are the same. That if I go into the one stillness within me, and then reach out to the greater stillness beyond, I meet in the stillness a power with no name. And in that nameless, silent power, I find that which I was missing in myself.

This I have found. . . . That many come to know that stillness, and they hold fast to it, they remain inside it. But I have found that to live as the Nameless would have us live, we need to find that stillness again and again, and go out from it, go out into the world again and again.

I could live in a hut or a cave, but the life of spirit is lived out in the world of people. So one must go into the stillness, but then turn back to the world again.

This I have found. . . . That the stillness heals. That the going into stillness heals. That the very trip of going toward the stillness heals, even if one does not find it right away. That often it is enough to look. That sometimes, especially with Spirit, the looking and the finding are the same.

This much I can say. . . . No one has to suffer, but suffering is a great teacher. In suffering I came to meet and to love my fellow sufferers. And in the meeting and in the loving, the suffering melted away. Some would say to drop the loving, to drop the meeting. But I say, all is of the Spirit. And in the meeting and in the loving, Spirit is only meeting and loving itself again.

I have come to see. . . . That the path of meeting is slow, that the path of discovering the stillness is a slow one also. But we meet what we need to meet as we push along through the trees. We meet small things when we are small, and bigger things as we grow larger. We meet what we need to meet. Whether we like it or do not like it.

This I know. . . . That as the drum beats, as the dancers dance, as the rhythm takes over and carries one deeper and deeper into Spirit, the world unfolds and we know our place in it. But we must hold fast to that knowing, and carry it back with us into morning. For as the cosmic ecstasy of darkness is, in the arms of a beloved, dark, deep, and vanished in a moment, so too is the memory of place in the midst of the dancing. A sudden burst of knowingness in the pit of the body-flesh. A washing out, and unfolding. Coming like a flood in a moment. And then gone again. Knowledge given, but difficult to carry. For all save those who go into the stillness. Then they, with empty hands, have strength to carry back the gifts of knowing that Spirit always gives. For it isn't that Spirit does not give. No. Spirit gives always. It is we who do not know how to carry away from that giving place that which is given.

I say. . . . That what I once learned in being in the flesh is no different than what I have learned in being among the dead. That one must keep going into the stillness and then dancing out again. That the dance of living and the dance of the so-called dead is not the same. But the stillness is. The stillness is always the same. It links all the worlds. And if you know it in the flesh, you will know it when the flesh is gone. You will know it to be the same. Familiar. A friend.

I want to tell. . . . About the way we spirits wait. Out of bodies, yet closer to the living than the living themselves. Waiting to talk, waiting to listen. Present, in great number. All of us present for communion.

Once the living and the dead were joined together in conversation. Then all the aspects of humanity were bound together like thongs around a bundle of kindling. But without listening to the spirits, there is no union. For ours are the voices that come to teach in the stillness. To teach what we see and what we have learned.

I want to say. . . . How beautiful, like morning, is the Spirit. Like night of stars and moment of rest. When the gray between the blue and the black makes its short, brief dance. And we too are like the gray: between worlds. Between blue and black, between shimmer and darkness. But so beautiful. Like breath and sigh of lover for friend. A drum. Coming to meet me in the dance, an understanding.

To some I have been a friend. To others I have been an adversary. But I have always been Akkub, always been myself. Knowing friend and adversary to be the same. To be the two aspects of my beingness. For we are all here to be teachers to each other. And we teach in many different ways. And only when we forget this do we hurt one another. And only when we forget this does suffering turn into pain.

I say. . . . I come to talk. I come as compassion. In this meeting, there is much for me. In touch and in remembering. So I come in love, and I go the same. For love is the stillness and love is the dance. Love is the Spirit and the Nameless. So I come and I go, and I too dance. Never very close, but never far away. As you turn in your dance, finding the answers that Spirit gives so freely when we learn to carry them.

*

NINIHWAH lived in the north, in Siberia, in the second century before the birth of the prophet Jesus. She was left by her family to die after a terrible illness infected her body, covering her skin with boils that ate her flesh away. So she was left alone, in a skin tent, to die. But instead, she entered into the nature of her illness—the anger she felt toward her husband for taking a second wife. In understanding her anger, she understood the anger of the world, and the fear of death confronting her faded away. So that she was content to die. And in her contentedness, she was healed of her illness and awakened to a sense of cosmic wholeness.

When her family returned a year later to gather up her remains and perform the appropriate rites, they found a vigorous woman, very much alive. They claimed a miracle. She claimed common sense. Her teachings began then, as she left her husband and family to wander and to heal. What she taught concerning enlightenment continued in the oral traditions of her people for centuries.

The basis of her message was as follows: "Move not ever anywhere but from the heart. Think not of anything that does not come from Oneness." And Ninihwah's presence today is especially concerned with healing.

Some Words of Ninihwah

People think the work is difficult. It is simple. So simple that everyone misses it. People think that sacrifice is required. But the gods do not want sacrifices. They do not need to be told how great they are. There is only one discipline, and only one ritual needed, so simple that only the most ancient among us remember it.

Close your eyes for a moment. Put your hands on your heart. Feel your heart beating and beat with it. Feel your heart beating and know that this very same beat is beating in the hearts of everyone you see, everyone you don't see. Know that this very same beat is beating in the hearts of all humans, all animals, beating even in the heart of the world itself.

Do this when you rise. Do this as you fall into the world of sleep. Do this when you are happy. Do this when you are sad. Do this when you are in love, and do this when you are in hate. Stop and place hands on your heart, and know that the beat you are feeling is the same beat that is beating in the heart of the one that you hate. Do this when you sit by the water. Do this for a moment when you sit beneath a tree to wipe the sweat from your brow on a day of good working. Do this when you are not working. Do this when you are lost and afraid. Feel the beat, and beat with it. This is the only practice that the gods require of humanity. For when you do this, everything else falls into place.

Take the hands of your babies and place them on their hearts. This and the love in your hands when you hold them is all the teaching babies need. I learned this in the cold when I was left to die, when I wanted to die. I placed my hands on my heart and I found life there. I beat with the beat, and I was reborn.

People think that what matters is what they believe. But the gods do not belong to any one religion. Or rather, they belong only to one religion—the religion of the heart. All is one in the heart. The work is that simple. All is one in the heart, and all hearts are one—the hearts of humans, planets, stars, gods, and the One that created all things. If there is need of healing, this is the only healing that there is. If there is need of balance, in body and in world, this is the only balancing act that there is. Once I was left to die, and instead I found eternal life. For even the dead have hearts, hearts that never once stop in their beating. And this is the only movement that there is. Not on or up, but only drumbeat beating of the heart of Oneness, beating through all of creation.

✳

CHIRAC lived among the Olmec of Mexico, in the days before the coming of the Spaniards. Alone, he journeyed from his family homeland to a peninsula overlooking the sea, the Atlantic. In his great quest for the god beyond gods, he was willing to wait a whole lifetime. But his solitude, and the need to survive—these basics of a simple life—deepened him so well that the opening came to him in two years' time.

When he returned to his homeland, he was so changed in mind and body that there could be no doubt of the validity of his experience. What he taught was remembered into the days after the coming of the Spaniards. Although much was lost, legends of his life remain among the old folk. They talk of one in whom the love of the whole world was united. One who held the sun and the moon and the planets inside him. One who gathered around him disciples, in order to teach them the mystery of the in-dwelling Cause. One who died of great old age, surrounded by grandchildren and great-grandchildren. One who never stopped loving the simplicity of life. A cool cup of water on a hot day. A beautiful sunset. All of this, resonating with wholeness. All of these hidden strands traveling back to the Source.

Some Words of Chirac

Lately, it seems to me, the world is changing. Time is changing, for the Earth is racing around the sun a little bit more quickly. With all this racing, it is hard to stay in control. So I say, fall out of control. Dance instead.

In my wanderings, there were times when I was filled with despair. To be human is a difficult path. Especially on a world that is always a little bit out of control itself. People think that saints are always in control, of their thoughts and of their emotions. This is not true. Only when you become rigid can you stay in control. And you only can stay in control that way until you fall over. True saints dance. They dip and bend and turn, in and out of all the joys and sorrows Earth gives to its children.

Sitting on a rock, be silent and try to feel the Earth spinning beneath you. People think the ancestors didn't know that the world was a sphere. But anyone who sits can feel it turning. Turning round the sun. Moon turning around it. So how can there be stability in the midst of this dance? It cannot happen.

The animals know this. They change with the seasons. People once knew this, and they are knowing it again. The world of power doesn't want you to know this. It wants you to go to work and make things no one needs, and offer services that serve no one. But when you let yourself change, change with the tilting of the Earth and with the seasons, then you come into a greater harmony, a harmony with many rhythms to it.

The first time I saw the sea, I thought to myself, "What a great thing this is." And the first time I really saw the stars, spinning and turning, I knew that the sea was very small. And yet the sea that came crashing at my feet is a mirror of the sea of heavenly clouds that made the stars. And the turning within me, isn't it the same as the turning of the axis of the universe itself?

To know the one and to know the many, to know that the One and the many are the same—that was where my teaching came from. It came from all my cells knowing, not just from my head. It came from all my body knowing, and when my body had all that knowing in it, then I, the soul that I am, then I too knew it, knew it because I was living in a body.

The body is the book in which we all read God. The body is the teaching. Winged spirits hover round us—because they learn from our bodies. The feathered ones are a still point in God, and we are the turning round the world's great axis. Be turning with the world. This is what God made us to be.

I sat once with my students. They wanted to hear words of wisdom. All that I could say to them was this. When you wake, every day, touch your body all over, from head to toe. Do this when you wake and do this when you fall asleep. Rub your body. Massage it. If you cannot touch every part, touch what you can. Touch your body as if you were your most perfect lover. You are what you have been looking for all this time. You are the doorway to the Great Beloved. You are the only doorway to the temple.

Most of my students did not want to hear this. They did not understand it. But that was a very long time ago. The world is changing. The world has changed. It changes in slow and subtle ways, but the world you are living in is not the same world that I last walked on. The air is poisoned, the water is poisoned, the Earth itself is ripped and scarred. But your souls, my friends, your souls—how wise they have become.

And the Earth can be healed. And the air can be healed, and the water can be healed. As more and more of you allow yourselves to really live as bodies in the world. There cannot be any separation any longer between matter and spirit, between soul and the body it creates for itself. Matter isn't less than spirit. It is spirit compacted, spirit made dense. So touch your body every day. Speak to all of your cells. Rejoice in the gift of life. Dance. Dance every day. This will heal everything.

※

DIHH-ANEH lived in an area of the world, now covered by water, that extended out from Madagascar. His enlightenment came early in the history of humanity. Like a single drum note, it echoed in the minds of all humanity, and served as a catalyst to the rest of humankind. Spreading a note of love, of oneness, of a rising upward and outward through experience into Spirit. His vision of thousands of years ago still has not been realized. A vision that transcends duality and exists in wholeness.

Dihh-Aneh is a guardian of our future direction, much as he stands at the portals of our past. His simplicity and nonverbal teachings, a reflection of his time, have nonetheless a great validity for us today, in an era of too much talking and too little said. What he taught by his movements, we can profit from in our time. With simplicity, fluidity, and ease.

Some Words of Dihh-Aneh

Wash your front door.
Fling wide your windows.
Go for a long walk—and look at Everything.

When you eat, taste the dirt your food grew in.
When you sit on the toilet, pray.

If you wake, be thankful.
When you do not wake, fly.
And step strong into the future.
If you walk on ants—they come right back.

※

IR-DA-KAH lived in northern Iceland, among the earliest people to find that land. He was only a child when he found enlightenment, a child of nine. Because he died only two years later, his teaching on this plane was brief. But in his wisdom, he found Oneness. And the illness that led him out of our physical life led him into a spiritual life of teaching that still goes on. For with enlightenment comes a desire to share it. With all living creatures. And this desire makes guides and companions of all enlightened beings. Women, men, and children.

Ir-da-kah was exceptional in his capacity to be aware, but the awareness that he reached at age nine is the same awareness any of us can reach at any time in our lives. For we are born out of Oneness, return into Oneness. And the only thing that keeps us from being fully aware of the Oneness all the time is ourselves.

Ir-da-kah is often the "imaginary" friend of little children with a spiritual gift, especially those little children who seem not to relate well to their peers.

Some Words of Ir-da-kah

Once, all the people in the world listened to those of us who only have bodies of light. Now, only children listen. And by the time they are seven, the door between our world and yours has been firmly shut. So I talk to everyone I can. I talk to them while they are floating in their mother's bodies. And I am not the only one. Hundreds and thousands of us are doing this talking. Talking when people will still listen. And if you listen, if you listen now, who will speak to you from somewhere else? Who walks with you? Who dreams with you and tries to reach you still when you are dreaming? Dreaming is the only place left where people still let us in.

Once there was a time when the living and the dead were always talking. I hope that time will come again. The living and the dead are the two hands of humanity. Together, we could make such wonderful things. I like to make things. I like to make dreams real. I could have come back and had a body again, but so many other people wanted to have bodies. And I had had enough to not be needing one again. But I am still a human being, still a part of the great living family of all human beings. I still have things to say, and if you sat quietly and talked to me, I would talk back to you. I, or one of my thousands of friends.

Most grown-ups do not play. When was the last time that you played? Did you play today? If you let yourself play again, your whole world would change. Everything would get lighter—your body, your work, your feelings. Ten minutes of real play a day could change the whole world. I know this. I know this for a fact. I know that there are other planets where people just like you grow up and still remember how to play. They play alone and they play together. They play with friends, friends you cannot see with those eyes of yours that see the sunlight. They have a good time playing, and so could you. Can you think of a single game to play with yourself? Can you play with the same sense of fun you used to feel when you were small? If you can do that, your whole world will change. If your whole world changes, everyone's whole world will change too. For the better. Maybe even for the best.

*

WANNAKAH was a Native American woman who lived on the eastern plains in the thirteenth century of the Western era. Her family were all healers and shamans, but it was in her striving for even deeper, wider meaning that she entered into a series of yearly retreats for a month in the summertime, when she could best leave her children and her family. Her annual retreats resulted, at the end of thirteen years, in her attaining complete enlightenment.

Were there no Spanish invasions, no displacement and up-heaval, Wannakah might be known today as the Buddha of the Western world. Instead she comforts in silence, in dreams, un-known to the people. But known by her compassion. For in her re-treat she found Oneness. Oneness of all life. Oneness of all people.

In dance she made her message known to the people. In story and song, she made her message known to the people. She taught a method of self-awareness that began with concentrating on the area of one's inner body just below and behind the navel. In dance and in work, she taught that when all movement begins in that place, one lives one's life in a centered way. And from cen-teredness, she taught, one moves out into awareness of the cos-mos. As a single individual who is nonetheless connected to all other people, past and present.

She taught of the need for choosing simplicity. She taught her followers a simple way of expressing their thanks to the Great Mystery Happening—by closing their eyes, breathing in deeply, and letting out their breath with a sigh of contentment from the center. This *ahhh*, she said, travels further than words of thanks-giving, for it comes from the whole of a person.

Her teachings were controversial in her own lifetime, for she was willing to teach anyone, of any tribe. But her compassion was such a tangible presence that one could not help but be moved by her, healed in ways in which one did not know one needed to be healed.

In her extreme old age she lived alone in a shelter, sat in the doorway, and greeted strangers. By her touch she healed. But her words, her stories, were strong. And after her death, she con-tinues to be a strong healer. A powerful teacher. Wannakah, a grandmother of the Center. Wannakah. To call on her is to seek union.

Some Words of Wannakah

I have come, and now I come again. I walk in silence, I walk in song. I walk in pain. I walk in beauty. Feet lightly to the Earth, I walk in all its Earth ways.

Come walk with me. Come walk with me in all the Earth ways. Deer, owl, bison, rattler—see how they walk with me, see how I walk with them.

Remember the old ways. Remember the ways so old that they come from the stars. Remember the worlds where everyone walked in harmony. Remember the worlds where all was beauty.

Feel the center in your body, the Earth center. Feel that there are sinews radiating out from this spot, connecting hands and feet and top of head to this center. Whenever you sit or bend, walk or swim, feel how you are like a star, the ends of you connected to this center. Close your eyes and feel it. When you move in the world, feel it.

When you move in the world in this way, you connect with the stars of the sky. When you move in the world in this way, the sky and the Earth are connected.

Animals do not ever lose their star-senses. People have not lost them, either. We have just turned away from them for a time. Turn back. It is time to turn back again. Turn back to the light of the stars that life comes from.

Breathe now. Breathe into your center. Breathe in and out. The breath of life this is. How often do you remember? Breathing into your center, breathing out. Breathing the Earth and the stars into your body, and letting them breathe you. Surrendering your breath and letting yourself be breathed. How often do you remember to do this? When you wake, when you walk, when you wander into sleeping again, stop for a moment to be one with your breathing.

I sing the breath of life. Wherever I gifted the people, this was the gift that I gave them—the song of the breath of life. Like a songbird, I come to you with this teaching. Into the center, the song of the center, the song of all of life.

Today I am walking the river of stars. I am walking and singing the song of the Earth. Of Earth, the perfect gem. Sparkling. See how Earth sparkles. See how you are part of this light. Breathe in the light. Breathe in all the light that there is. Fire and wood and stone and herbs—they make a pipe. Breathing the light of stars and Earth in, you make of your body a pipe.

Once my people lived in harmony with the Earth and with the stars. Now you are remembering how to live in harmony with all that is. Walk in harmony. Sing in harmony. Sing the song of life. Walk in harmony. Sing in harmony. This is the breath of life.

Walk with me now in the joy ways. Sing with me now in the Earth ways. Breathe with me now in the star ways. All ways are one. In and out. All ways are one. Even the Creator breathes, whole universes, in and out.

Once I walked the Earth, and now I walk the stars. Once I breathed the air of Earth and now I breathe the air of stars. Walk with me. Breathe with me. Make of your body a pipe and breathe with me. Walks-pipe. Sings-pipe. Peace-pipe. Holy.

✳

AH-HI-NA-AE lived in the sixteenth century of this era in the Marshall Islands. Her female ancestors had all been fire priest-esses, and her awakening came to her in her service to the fire goddess. Her vision was pure and transcendent. She saw the god-world as the merest reflection of the absolute formless Oneness, where fire and sea are united in a harmony that preexists duality and is nonetheless still present. In serving the fire goddess she discovered the way to go beyond the gods. For her way was one of stillness and waiting. And what she taught was a way of living with waiting, by reminding oneself constantly of the Oneness of all things. Till the awakening comes.

Some Words of Ah-hi-na-ae

I raise my hands in joy. Raise your hands. Be thankful for your existence. From Nothing the Creator made life. Be thankful for life. It is a gift.

I raise my voice in joy. Raise your voice. Be thankful for your existence. From Nothing the Creator made worlds. Be thankful for your world. It is a gift.

I raise up my spirit in joy. Raise your spirit. Be thankful for your existence. From Nothing the Creator made experience. Be thankful for experience. It is a gift.

I raise up my soul in joy. Raise up your soul. Be thankful for the joy that holds all things together. From Nothing the Creator made joy. From Nothing the Creator made joy that holds all universes together. Feel the joy, wherever you are. Feel the joy, holding even your sorrow together. Raise up your soul and know that it is made from joy. Be thankful for the joy, even when you do not always see it. It is a gift. It is a gift. It is a gift.

❋

NARAZ was a poet who lived among a tribe of seminomadic people in the Lake Van area, in the fifteenth century. His method of making music was to go into trance. And from out of the trance states came a series of song cycles that told of the stages of awakening.

A wanderer with a self-imposed vow of poverty and chastity, he surrounded himself with no followers. Sang to anyone who would listen. And took as his reward the simple pleasure of his gift of clarity.

In his lifetime his songs were remembered. One hundred years later they were all but forgotten. He sang about dancing into wisdom. His gentleness resulted in a violent death by attack. But he died singing, and singing he still is, on the spirit plane. As guide and teacher. To those who seek inner music.

Some Words of Naraz

Through the opening of my tent
fly angels.
Their eyes are emerald.
Their wings are on fire.

I long to burn in their embrace.
Through the opening of my tent
fly angels.
Their hearts are made of snow.
I long to drink of the cool cool melting waters.
But how can this be,
wings of fire, hearts of unmelted snow?
The Creator is mysterious.
I am a fool.
Fool vision, Naraz.
Angels do not fly through the opening of your tent.
They are always here.

The mountain is old.
Goats know it intimately.
Their voices echo from canyon to canyon.
How like a goat I have been.
Leaping from crag to crag.
Only, goats do not look to the summit.
I do not stop yearning.
Naraz, since the day you were born,
you have been a person.
Naraz, since the time of your conception,
you have been a person.
Some say, "Give up desire. Be where you are."
I wish that I could be a goat.
But since the time of my first breath,
I have always been a person,
looking to the tops of mountains.

Yesterday, I was gathering roses.
The thorns that did not prick me
took offense.
They want to prick.
Finally, I let one.
In return, the rose let me lean my face into its bliss.
Rapture.
There is nothing

in that moment when your nose is filled
but heaven.
I have heard that there are scentless roses.
What greater offense could there be
against the Earth, Naraz,
if the thorns have nothing to protect?

Dancing, I broke my ankle.
I twisted it in the dirt.
That hole, I wanted to destroy it.
But a hole is empty already.
That pain, I wanted to destroy it.
But it said to me, "Naraz,
I didn't make the hole.
I didn't make the bone.
A clumsy poet
can still make words."
So I sit on this bed of pain,
my leg wrapped and splinted,
and I sing.

*

DOURG lived in ancient India, centuries before the Aryans became the rulers of the subcontinent. Her enlightenment came to
her slowly, over the years—not in a single flash or burst of light. It
came to her so slowly that she could never say when she was,
and when she wasn't, aware of the Divine.

She lived her life as a potter. And even in the years when
women and men gathered before her house to listen to her speak,
with hands on wheel she spun out pots and painted them. Talking of the thunder of life that filled her mind when she turned inward. Some were made wise by her words. Many more were
made wise just from watching her, and seeing the possibility of
awareness in the flesh.

To call upon her in your work is to gain a blessing from her.
The dead are not gone. They have simply changed their locus.

Some Words of Dourg

The clay is the Earth. The clay is my body. Each time hands sink down into it, they sink deep into my heart. The images in my heart—they are beautiful. How long will it take me to make them? A thousand lifetimes could go past. A single moment. All of this is the same when my hands are in the clay.

The trees make acorns. The birds make nests. The is the work the Mother has given me. All She created, She created to work in her garden. The birds make nests, the ants build cities. There is no difference between a human and an ant. Oh yes, there is. Each morning when it wakes, ant remembers its dreams. Each morning when it wakes, human forgets them.

The clay is the Earth. I am from the Earth. Each morning when I sit by my wheel, I remember my dreams. How do you remember your dreams? How do you shape them into the day? This is all I ask of you. The rest is your work, this remembering and this making.

✳

INUBU lived in East Africa, in the region that is today known as Uganda. Her realization of Oneness was a gradual process in which she overcame the massive disabilities she was born with, which necessitated her being carried in a sling chair for the greater part of her life. She overcame the disabilities by using those very same limitations to free her mind to enter realms that others, in their "normality," could not reach.

The clarity of her initial awakening, and the many smaller experiences that followed, slowly gave her the spiritual strength to heal herself from a crippling form of arthritis and then move on, in order to teach not only healing, but awareness as well.

The lines of women healers that she began continued uninterrupted for thousands of years in the east and the center of Africa, from her day, when the first kings in Egypt were ruling a united land, down through the ages till time and history erased her lineage. But on the spirit plane her work goes on. Her work of guiding.

Some Words of Inubu

People say one thing is holy and another thing isn't. People say one day is special and another day isn't. What would happen, my dears, if you lived in the world in such a way that everything you did, you did knowing it was holy; if you lived in the world knowing that every day was a sacred day?

When you wash your dishes and they are holy. When you brush your teeth knowing they are holy. When you pray or meditate with the same sense of doing something holy. When you talk to your friends on the phone knowing they are holy. When you talk to the cashiers in the supermarket knowing they are holy. When you drive in your car in a holy way. When you throw out your garbage in a holy way. When you wash your clothing in a holy way, knowing that the soap, the water, and the clothes themselves are holy. When the washing machine is holy, and you know it. When the dryer is holy, and you know it. When you take out your clothes and fold them with the same reverence that priests and priestesses of old used to fold and put away their vestments—then the world will be what it was intended to be. And you will be who you were intended to be—fully present in your bodies, and wholly holy.

It can take a thousand lifetimes to get to this place. But how many lifetimes do you think you've had? None of you were born yesterday. All of you are older than you think. And I have watched human history. And many of you think that nothing has changed—that, in fact, everything has gotten worse. But I do not see it that way. I see a greater and greater rising into consciousness of more and more human beings. And I rejoice in this movement in spirit, remembering a time when I could not move myself.

Today is not easy. Tomorrow may not be easy. But if you all hold fast to the visions you came in with, those visions will become real. If you reach out to us for support and for guidance, we will support you and guide you.

I see how people turn to this or that book, to this or that teacher. Some laugh, seeing them wander from school to school, from discipline to discipline. Some criticize themselves, for not being able to find in one place what they are looking for. But I celebrate when I see this. I celebrate anyone who is looking. For the more you look and do not find exactly what you are looking for, the more you will discover that there is no one out there who can teach you what you want to know. For you have all lived in many different times and places. You have all lived as women and men. So there is no one teaching that can show you every part of who you are. But there are many out there who can guide you back into remembering that everything you need to know you can find within your heart. I mean this literally. The human heart is made in such a way that it can give you access to all wisdom. Like a radio or a television, the heart can be so tuned that it picks up information directly, picks up everything you are capable of knowing.

When you live each day in holiness, the cells become holy again. When the cells are holy again, the information-receiving device that the human body is begins to operate as it was intended to operate by the One who created it. When the cells are holy, the heart is holy—the heart of this receiving and transmitting device. When the heart is holy, it can access everything you need to know. Then there will be no more teachers, for everyone will be a teacher, everyone will be each other's teachers. And the world will be made whole again. And the great experiment in consciousness that has been happening on this beautiful planet will unfold in beauty and in wisdom.

Everyone who is here now is a part of this experiment. Everyone who has chosen to come here in this time is a part of the unfolding of this experiment. Long have we been working to get to this place. And near is the day of celebration.

All is One. And in the Oneness are many voices. Let us all sing together. The holy day of transformation is at hand.

※

TUGALANIKAK lived in ancient Australia long before the coming of the European invaders. He was the heir to a long tradition of healing workers. But he took his spiritual powers and entered into a deeper state of awareness where his personal self was eradicated and his sense of Oneness was constant.

Through his sense of Oneness he could induce deep states of dreams in his followers, through which they themselves could experience some of what he had experienced in his own opening.

From there the path was easier for them, and they too in time often became enlightened.

Living as he did on the edge of the God-world, he could channel back into this world the pure light of Spirit that nurtures our hearts and souls as spiritual pilgrims in this world. To those who did not understand him, his power was frightening. But those who knew his way saw not power, but emptiness filled with light. Not the light of a person, but a light divine.

Some Words of Tugalanikak

Stay close to the Earth. Let your feet be always your teachers, your hands be always your students, and let your heart be the rhythm you dance to.

Stay close to the Earth, no matter how covered over it is by concrete and buildings and cities. For just beneath that skin, the Earth always is, alive and throbbing.

Wherever you are, whenever you are, stop as a meditation, and simply feel the Earth-beat we were all born into. This is the source of all music, this is the source of all life.

Just as our heartbeat comes from the Earth, its heartbeat comes from the sun, and its heartbeat comes from the heart of this galaxy, and its heartbeat comes from the heart of this universe, whose heartbeat comes from the heart of the One who has made all things. And all of these hearts, all of these hearts are beating together, beating as one.

Stay close to the Earth. Old man Earth, weary and hungry and much in need of healing. Feed him, this old man. Lie close to his old-man skin and let him feel your heart beating down into his.

Stay close to the Earth. Let your feet be your only teachers, taking you everywhere you go, letting you go everywhere you need to go.

The people of the sea are footless. That is their destiny. They swim the liquid body of this old man Earth. They swim in his eyes, in his blood, in his body. As they swim, you walk, you walk and keep walking.

These feet of yours—honor them. Touch them with your hands and say, "Feet, tell me all the Earth has told you, when you whisper quietly together." Walk without shoes whenever you can. Let your feet know the Earth again, as lovers know each other's bodies— soft, hard, intimate. Together.

In the time when all the animals and all the people still spoke to- gether—in that time, when feet were still new as a way of meet- ing, and talking, and loving, all the world was still together then.

Be all the things; be rocks and trees and fish and insects and birds and animals. Be whatever you see, be it for a moment, friend or foe. This is why old man Earth made you, made hu- mans—so that one part of him could become all the other parts. For he was getting old, too old to still be all of them himself.

Be all the things. Be everything you see. It is for this that old man Earth made you, humans. Made one part of himself that could weave together all the other pieces.

Let yourself be always weaver, weaving together all that you see. Weaving together all that you see into the fabric of who you are as yourself. Be that part of the Earth that is always weaving all the other pieces together. Wherever your feet carry you, be weav- ing together all that you see.

Reach out those hands. Reach out those hands that are always new. Whatever you touch, touch it for the first time. Old man Earth shaped these hands for you so that some part of his body could always be young again, feeling everything for the first time. So feel everything, and feel it be new. Do this for yourself, and do this for the world that made you.

Not all worlds make people as this world has. Some worlds are silent and alone with themselves. But old man Earth, he wanted noise, he wanted dance, he wanted song to cover his skin, to beat with him, to play with him, to play all the rhythms that ever were and ever will be. So honor this world that made you, that made all of life. Sing. Dance. Make all the music you can. Make all the music you can make between your feet and your hands. This is the way to weave all things together.

Once there was a time when things were new. They were new and everything had to be tried out. Once people were new. And they had to try everything. Now people are old. Each one has lived in many different bodies. So it isn't enough to be everything you see. You must be everyone you ever were, too.

Sit, quietly, and remember. Remember through your feet how many times you have walked this planet. Your head will not tell you this. But your feet will. Wherever you walk, they will say, "I have been here before. I have been here walking."

How long can you walk? How long can you walk and not remember all of who you are? For you are everyone. Every man. Every woman. Everyone who has ever walked on two feet on this old-man planet, that is who you are. Walking.

Once there was a time when a foot could touch the Earth for the first time. Sink down in sand or soil where no one had ever been before. But feet of humanity cover the Earth now. Feel them. They are your feet. And all that they know is who you are.

Feel your breath. Now stop. Hold it. Hold it for as long as you can. Be in the moment when you have to breathe again. That moment, that moment is all of you calling out to the body of flesh that you made for the spirit and soul of yourself.

Stop. Hold your breath. Hold it for as long as you can. And be in that moment when you have to take in breath again. Be in the moment and be in the breath. That is who you are, beyond the body and beyond the breath.

The parent of light is darkness, the mother of all things. Be in the darkness of the moment when you have to take a breath, when your body has to breathe itself. As your body does, so too the Earth did when it made a body for itself, when it made the rocks and trees and fish and all the other people.

People. How many other people? Can you count them? Old man Earth was busy making people. No one could count them. Not even he. He did not want to count them. He wanted only to make them. He wanted to make all of them. And then he made you to be them all. Be all of them. And even you cannot count them.

Once, when people were new, shamans and healers were the only ones who could be everything. They were old then. They were old before everyone else. But now everyone is old. Old of foot and able to be everything.

No one is older than anyone else anymore. Remember that. Everyone is just as old. Because everyone is one, together.

You want to be young. But I say, be old again. Be old together. There is so much joy in being old. Yes, say that. Say that out loud for yourself: "There is so much joy in being old. There is so much joy in being old together."

The sun is old, and yet it hasn't stopped giving out light. Old Grandmother Sun is old. And all of her children are old. But that has not stopped them from dancing round her old-woman body.

Once there was a time when all the stars were new. Now they are old. Not very old. Not very very old. Just old. Good old. Rich old. Not yet even ripe old.

I remember a time when people were new. Even then the Earth was old. But people were new. In all of that newness, there wasn't enough room to hold all the light. No, you have to be old and stretched out a bit to hold all the light that you want to hold inside yourself. This is the pleasure of being old. To be stretched out enough, to be strong enough of years that everyone can carry all the light there is. Carry it from the sun. Carry it for the Earth.

Be old for the Earth. Do not do it just for yourself. Do it for Earth, too. That is what all of us know, who are old teachers. However long it has been since we have lived in physical bodies, we live in bodies still, bodies that come from the Earth. And in these spirit bodies, this is what we all know. How loving a father the Earth has been. To have made of himself all these bodies.

Be old in your body. Do it for Earth, too. Feel the oldness of Earth through your feet. Feel the allness of Earth through your eyes. Feel the newness of Earth through your hands. Feel the light of Earth in your heart. And know that the light of Earth is the sun's light, being carried. That you carry the Earth's light, as he carries sun, as she carries light from the place of her birthing.

Once there was a time when people were new. People were new on this Earth, still mostly animal. But something had been cut in people, cut by Father Earth away from all the other animals. They were new, just learning how to see as humans see. And there was one of them, one who could see the rocks and be rock, the trees and be trees. And this one, Djigi—this one could see not only the things that could be seen, but the things that could be dreamed. This one was the first human dreamer. And Djigi dreamed awake. And Djigi dreamed how much light there is. And Djigi held all the light that is in the darkness of dreaming. And that one, that one Djigi—she was the first one to ever be in-light-filled. That one Djigi was the first one ever on the planet to take in all the light that is, in a human way—that Djigi.

While you are here, be here. Like Djigi. When you are gone, be gone. But now you are here.

While you are alive, be alive. Like Djigi. When you are not alive, we will be here to meet you, in this here, this other earthly here. With Djigi. For even this here away from form is Earth's here, Earth's spirit, Earth's whole aliveness.

While you are here, let the Earth be your teacher. Moment by moment, honor all that he has made. While you are alive, let the body be your teacher. Earth body. Light body. One body. Holy.

PART TWO

GROUNDING
WISDOM IN
YOUR BODY
AND YOUR LIFE

Chapter 6

READING THE WISDOM
IN YOUR BONES

D oes it seem odd to you that I have gone from talking
about the spiritual roots of human history to a section
on bones? Bear with me, because you will soon see
how deeply connected the two are. For the journey we
have been on for the last two million years has been about
creating bodies evolved enough for our souls to fully manifest in. And it's the bones that are the armature for our
bodies.

"I knew it in my bones," we sometimes say, about a
feeling so deep that it goes beyond words. This expression
is not just a turn of phrase, but, as you shall see in the
section that follows, a reflection of what is deeply true
about ourselves.

We are immortal souls dancing through space and
time. Often we forget this, but again and again teachers
from the great Earth University have incarnated to remind us that that is so. One of them, Jesus of Nazareth,
told his followers, "The kingdom of God is within you."
In other words, we do not have to turn outward to find

wisdom, for everything we need is already within us now—peace, love, joy, and meaning.

Scientists may peer into our DNA, looking for the secret of who we are, but they will never find it. For what is encoded within us by our souls that makes us unique is patterned in nonatomic matter in the matrix of our bones. When we turn there, deeply into our bones, we can find all the wisdom we seek, we can find the divine realm, the kingdom and queendom of heaven. For all of human wisdom is filed within us in our bones.

This information was given to me by one of my Earth University advisers, a wise woman named Tabbad, whose area of expertise in the Red College (she jokingly calls herself a red witch) is the mechanics of incarnation, and specifically, the way in which each soul encodes energy and information in a physical body. This material is useful both for expansion and for self-diagnosis. Bones that are broken or diseased indicate areas where we may be out of balance.

I always knew that bones had a deep significance, but it wasn't until 1992 that I finally opened up to this material. I spent the next three and a half years writing down this information and exploring it, a bone at a time, in myself and with others. I offer it to you now, a simple tool for self-exploration and soul wisdom.

❋　　❋　　❋

What Is Bred in the Bones

You may think of your soul as something small that lives within your body, perhaps in your heart. But in truth it is the body that lives within the vast sea of its soul. From the time of conception, each soul works with the growing structure of its chosen physical body, shaping it, guiding its unfolding, and encoding within its bones vast amounts of soul information.

How the soul does this work is by "stepping down" its current, first into the subtle bodies, and then through them into the physical body.

If you go back through time you will see that your ancestors knew this about the human body. The earliest burials, tens of thousands of years ago, were not just a way of showing reverence for the dead. The earliest cemeteries were libraries in which the bones of the dead were preserved so that their descendants could "read" them. Religions as diverse as Tibetan Buddhism and Catholicism have treasured the bones of their saints. Although they have forgotten how to read these relics, they have not forgotten that bones carry energy and information after death—information being patterned energy, different strands of it encoded by different individuals, each of whose bones is also imprinted with everything he or she learned in that particular life.

In fetuses, in newborns, and in children, the bones are not yet fully formed. In fact, the process of encoding continues for many years, as the soul imprints information in the bones that will be of use in a given incarnation. In ancient times, rites of passage were held to celebrate a child's entry into adulthood. These celebrations occurred when most of the bones were fully formed, which is when the soul completes its imprinting. When that has happened, a person is ready to go out into the world and make use of the knowledge he or she carries. As you continue through life, your bones continue to store new information, just as computer chips do.

The Structure of Bones

Your body has more than two hundred bones in it. Bones have many functions. They support and protect your internal organs, offer leverage for your muscles that allows you to move, and are the growth site for blood cells and other nutrients. The bones in a living person contain three layers: (1) the outer membrane layer, which is riddled with blood vessels and connects your bones to your ligaments and tendons; (2) the dense, mineral-rich layer, which is encoded by your soul; and (3) a porous inner section, which in your long bones contains bone marrow.

Look at the drawings of the bones of the human body, and familiarize yourself with them. Learn the names and locations of all your bones. Use the charts as an interior mirror, so that you can feel your bones within your body and get to know them. Feel them as they turn, move, and support you. Begin to see yourself as a living being that already contains within itself the image of death: a skeleton. Feel the strength and support this skeleton gives you, and begin to feel that it also contains a wealth of soul information that you are about to make conscious for yourself.

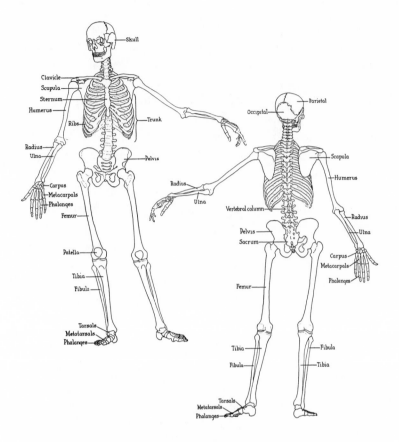

Accessing Information from Your Bones

When you are familiar with all the bones in your body, both from studying them externally and from touching and feeling them within yourself, you will be ready to learn how to "read" them.

The process of bone reading is quite simple. It happens by turning your consciousness inward.

Every bone in the body contains distinctive information. In bones that are paired, as most bones in the body are, this information is imprinted in duplicate. For example, whatever is stored in your left clavicle is also stored in your right clavicle. But just as our genes contain a double helix of information, it is through "reading" or "listening" to both bones at the same time, in stereo, that the information encoded in them will best be made conscious.

Once you know what is stored in your bones, you can read

the ones that carry the particular information you are looking for. Being able to do this will both ground you in your body and allow you to answer for yourself the kinds of questions you often present to other people: Who am I? Why was I born? What did I come here to accomplish?

What follows is a simple technique that will allow you to read your own bones.

1. Sit or lie quietly, in a place where you will not be interrupted. Dim the lights. Let the room you are in be silent.

2. Feel your breath rising and falling. Be one with your breath. Allow your entire body to move with your breath, slowly and gently. With soft and long inhalations and exhalations, let yourself begin to slow your breath down a bit, almost as if you were drifting into sleep.

3. Become aware of the bone (or bone pair) that you want to read. Place your hands over it if you can. If it is an internal bone, place your hand or hands over the area where it is found. Be aware of its shape and size. Deepen into it and feel it within you.

4. Now imagine a beautiful sky-blue light gathering all around you, a light that you can breathe right into your body, right into the bone or bones you want to read. You may even want to use a blue lightbulb as an aid in doing this. Breathe in the light till you can see the bone clearly inside you.

5. As the bone begins to glow within you, use sound to activate the stored information. Begin humming the sound *oh* out loud, and gradually allow the sound of your hum to spiral into your body until it deepens into the bone you want to read.

6. As you continue to chant, feel the shape of the bone, its size and thickness, as if you were holding it, turning it around, feeling every part of it with your mind's hands.

7. Now move your consciousness all the way into the bone, so that you enter it fully and become one with it, as if you had taken it into your wise and knowing heart.

8. Know that you can activate all of the information encoded within the bone. At this point you may want to let the sound become a silent vibration, rather than making it out loud.

9. Now, focus on the particular information you are looking for in this bone. Ask the question of this bone that you have come to it to ask.

10. Let this information rise up into your conscious mind. It may come in words, pictures, memories, feelings, hunches, smells, and so forth. Be present with the bone and with your capacity to receive information from it. You may want to have paper nearby so that you can record what you receive.

The Bone Dictionary

The Bones of Your Trunk

The RIBS are the <u>Fingers of Possibility bones</u>. It is into the ribs that your soul imprints all the manifold possibilities that it was created to explore. Each soul is different in this regard, and your ribs are encoded with the possibilities that are utterly unique to you. Some of these have been explored in other lives and other realities, and they are always there to inspire you now.

Place your hands on your rib cage, and see your ribs glowing pale blue inside your body, sheltering your heart and lungs and other organs. Do the chant as you tune your inner senses deep into your ribs. Let information surface in your conscious mind. Play your mind over the possibilities your soul was created to explore that were encoded in your ribs, just as your hands might play over a xylophone, making sound.

If you are at a point in your life when you feel stuck, at a crossroads, in transition, in need of change, this may be a good time to access the information in your ribs. And if you want to celebrate your vast potential as a living being, explore your ribs too. Notice how the information changes from lower to higher ribs. Be with all of your ribs all at once, and you will be filled with your own immortal possibilities now focused in the world of form.

The SCAPULA, or shoulder blades, are the Shape of Dream bones. Irregular in form, floating on your back above your ribs, these two paired bones contain your soul's highest dreams for you in this life. But it is important to remember that dreams are not the same as possibilities. Some dreams are not meant to be lived out; rather, they are supposed to be dreamed out, to nurture and inspire you. If you were an angel, your wings would attach here.

If you are lacking in vision, feeling spiritually shut down, finding yourself disconnected from your deepest source of inspiration, journey into your shoulder blades, and allow yourself to bask in your own soul's dreams. They may be too vast for you to make manifest in the world of form, but let your dreams feed you, be your muse.

The CLAVICLE, or collarbones, are the Joy in Form bones. Connected to the scapulae and the breastbone, floating over the ribs, the collarbones contain your soul's love of physicality, its joy in the limitations that living in a physical body imposes upon it. Limitation is what makes a sonnet. Limitation is the difference between two spirits meeting in the spirit world and interpenetrating, and two lovers meeting in the world of form and embracing each other, kissing each other.

Babies often cry because they have been drifting out of their body and find themselves suddenly back in it. If your baby is crying in this way, lightly rub one of its collarbones. If the baby in you wants to know what will bring it joy in this life, allow yourself to deepen into these bones and explore what you find there.

The STERNUM, or breastbone, is the Presence of Self in the World bone. For astrologers, it is your rising sign that tells something about how you present yourself to others. This bone contains your soul's choices about the ways it will present itself in the world. Attitudes and feelings are here. Desires are here.

If you are feeling confused about how others see you, or about how you want to be seen, read this bone. If you are feeling as if you have no protection, no natural defenses, or if you are feeling trapped in your own bulletproof shield, deepen into your sternum. When you need protection, feel this bone. When you need to present yourself in the world in a clear and self-directed way, feel this bone.

The Bones of Your Spine

The VERTEBRAE, SACRUM, and COCCYX make up the spine or backbone. We in the Earth University call them the Story of Self bones. The backbones contain the information your soul has imprinted in your body about your genetic history. The lineage of your ancestors is recorded here, as is the history of the human race, in the different parts of your spine.

Your *coccyx,* or tailbone, at the very tip of your spine, consists of several small fused bones and contains specific information about the earliest ancestors of the human species. .

The *sacrum,* at the base of your spine, is formed of five bones that fuse around age thirty. It contains information about the particular history of the human species, its evolution and development on the physical level, along with the wisdom the human species acquired as it grew.

There are three divisions of vertebrae. The five *lumbar vertebrae* are encoded with the history of your own particular genetic ancestors. Reading them will tell you more than photographs or family trees. They will anchor you and ground you in the world, give you all the support you need. You chose your particular family for a reason, and these bones will tell you what that is.

Each of the lumbar vertebrae contains a different field of information. The numbers start at the bottom of your spine and move up toward your head, going from higher to lower.

L5: relation to place, environment, feelings about home

L4: attitudes toward family and others, friend or foe

L3: feelings and attitudes toward children and parenting

L2: information about vocation and abilities

L1: family genetic hopes and dreams

The twelve *thoracic vertebrae,* to which your ribs are attached, have been imprinted by your soul with the information of your own past lives and soul history. Here are stored skills and talents and abilities that you have made use of and explored in other lives, to be used by you now whenever you tap into them. This information is encoded not in stories about your past lives, but in hard data accumulated from past experiences explored in physicality.

T12: basic survival skills

T11: vocational skills and talents particular to you

T10: information about gender and mating patterns

T9: overall life visions of your soul

T8: family, kinship, friendship, and intimacy information

T7: range of belief systems, religions explored

T6: personal beliefs, private individual philosophy

T5: range of feelings, anger, intensity of emotions

T4: collective life goals and how they are handled

T3: mechanisms for coping with limitation and failure

T2: capacity for exaltation and cosmic connection

T1: sense of self

The seven *cervical vertebrae* in your neck have been encoded with innate and accumulated soul skills that you have chosen to use in this particular life. Wrapping your hands around your neck and deepening into these bones will allow you to access these skills whenever you need them.

C7: self as aspect of God awareness

C6: particular goals established for this life

C5: capacity for vision, dreams, self-expansion

C4: limitations, challenges

C3: participation in the planet's unfolding

C2: relation to chosen body, its unfolding, its health

C1: experience of God and Unity, and how to explore them

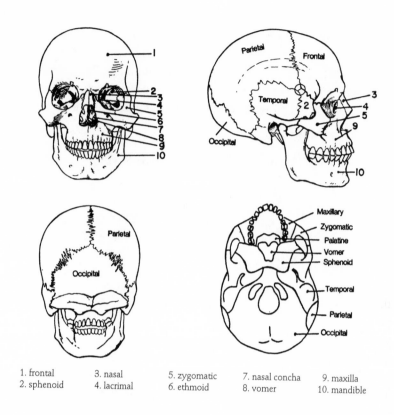

1. frontal
2. sphenoid
3. nasal
4. lacrimal
5. zygomatic
6. ethmoid
7. nasal concha
8. vomer
9. maxilla
10. mandible

The Bones of Your Skull

The skull is not just one bone but a complex puzzle of inter-locking shapes, some internal and others just below your skin. Some are paired and others are single. All of them are programmed with different information. Altogether there are twenty-five bones in your skull, not fully formed in newborns, that seem rigid in adults but in fact move throughout your life, softly coming to-gether and moving apart, a living jigsaw puzzle in the round.

As its name indicates, the FRONTAL bone forms the forehead. It is composed of two bones that gradually fuse around age six, although they remain joined by cartilage in about 10 percent of the adult population. This large curved bone is known to us as the Cup of Self bone. All of us, embodied and disembodied, have many different aspects. We have lived many different lives, been female and male, and carry all that knowledge with us. But there

is a singular and focal sense of self—a sense that "this is me"—
that all of us must have if we are to function. The sense of self, of
me, is imprinted by your soul in your frontal bone.

Think about what you do when you make a mistake, when
you step away from your Self. You cup your forehead, slap it,
wrap your palm around it. What are you doing but coming back to
your sense of self again? And when you do this consciously, the
wealth of information you receive from your soul increases vastly.

On either side of your head, behind the frontal bone, are the two
PARIETAL bones. These large domed plates over most of the top
of your head are known to us as the Shelter of Heaven bones. It
isn't just that they protect you from having your brain bashed in;
they also shelter within you your capacity for self-protection.
Hands to the top of your head is a gesture of shielding, and one
that prisoners are often forced to take. While from a law enforcer's
point of view this posture makes your hands visible and prevents
you from using any weapons, from the soul's point of view this
gesture is allowing you to access your own safety.

These are your boundary markers, the bones that contain the
information that will tell you how you are separate and different
from all other souls swimming in the vast ocean of All That Is.
Boundary stones, shelter; when you know these things about
yourself, then you are safe.

At the back of the head is the OCCIPITAL bone. This bone cups
the rear of your head, and you can locate it by finding the bump
back there. This magical bone has a large hole in it through which
your spinal cord passes and is known as the Tone of Your Presence bone. In other words, this bone contains the regulatory vibration that keeps you, your soul, your energy body, and all of
your physical cells in tune with each other. When you are feeling
out of sorts, out of kilter, out of harmony with who you are, all
you have to do is fill this bone with your own conscious mindful-
ness and you will easily be able to realign yourself with your
Self—the immortal child of God that you are. Cup the bump—
called the occipital protuberance—to align yourself with your
Self, and also to integrate any new information you are taking in.

Hold it with the tips of your fingers and gently turn it like a knob to put yourself back into harmony. Truly this cup of a bone is a marvelous tool for self-balancing in challenging times. (And what times are not challenging?)

On each side of your head are two bones called TEMPORAL bones. People often rest the tips of their fingers there and rub when they are in distress. Why? Because these two bones are the Walls of Healing bones. All living organisms move from balance to imbalance and back to balance again. There are many self-healing mechanisms in your body, but tuning into these bones will provide you with information from the soul level about what you can do to bring your body back into balance.

The two small NASAL bones at the top of your nose sit side by side. People grasp them and rub them when they are stuck in thought, for these bones are encoded with particular information that has given them the name Seat of Activation bones. When you tap into these bones, what you will find here is how to activate yourself, how to motivate yourself, how to turn yourself on. Tiny as they are, these bones are powerful. They are the on switch for action in every area of your life.

The paired bones that give structure to the front of your face are known as the MAXILLA. Your upper teeth are rooted in these bones. When you are being tuned and imprinted by your soul, what is impressed in these two bones has given them the name House of Wonderment bones. Your own individual sense of wonder, the things that make you say *ooh* and *aah*, that thrill and amaze and intrigue you, are stored here. This is the seat of all that you can sink your teeth into in the cosmos. So if you are feeling lusterless and disconnected from the splendors of creation, if you have done it all and have lost a sense of awe, tap into these bones, rest the tips of your fingers on them lightly, and let the shimmering sense of wonder that is uniquely yours begin to slowly awaken in your body and rise up into consciousness.

The bottom of your eye sockets and the inner arch of your cheekbones are formed by the maxilla bones, and the outer edges of your eye sockets and cheekbones are formed by the ZYGO-MATIC bones, or cheekbones. These elegantly curved structures are known to us as the Vessels of Meaning bones. Each life, each single incarnation, has a purpose, a meaning that emerges from the soul's immortal nature striving to express itself in the physical realm. Every life has meaning at every moment, however meaningless it might seem to others or to the one living it. These marvelous flared bones are my favorite in the human body. When you connect with them you will be hearing your own individualized version of *yes*, echoing into every cell of who you are. Rub them, hold them, place the tips of your fingers on them whenever you are feeling lost and uncertain, feeling like everything you are doing has no purpose. Tune into these bones and come back to your soul's own meaning, to your life's own meaning, encoded into your body for as long as your bones exist.

Behind your nose, forming part of the walls of your nasal cavity, you will find the ETHMOID bone. This singular structure cannot be felt from the outside, but it can be known through your inner senses of sight, hearing, touch. Find this bone and get to know it. We call it the House of No! bone. A curious name for a curious bone, called this not because there is no way to touch it from outside, but because the wisdom stored here is your ability to say no to things in life. This bone evolved its function from simple biological function: the ability to know what to eat and what to say no to. In simple life-forms this bone carries that task. In evolved human beings it carries that task out into all realms of thought and action. To know how to say no is a vital part of life, and if you have lost that capacity, tune into this lovely bone.

A part of the space between your two nostrils, the VOMER is a fascinating creature. We call it the Shaft of Discrimination. Distinguished from the function of the ethmoid bone, but equally important, this bone does not carry your soul's ability to make value judgments (good—yes; bad—no), but it makes distinctions based on a sense of what would be appropriate for you in a given situation. For example, something you eat when you are healthy may not be good for you when you are sick. This is different from knowing that something is never good for you. Tuning into the vomer will allow you to exercise discrimination, not just in the department of eating, but in every area of your life.

Shaped like a bird or a bat, flying at the base of your skull, the SPHENOID bone is called the Wings of Truth and Beauty bone. This marvelously formed bone in your head is the source of encoded information on the qualities of truth and beauty. Today, when so much of the world is scarred by ugliness in things done by and in things created by human beings, when truth is hard to find anywhere, I hope you find it comforting to know that all you need to do to find these qualities is to turn inward. There, truth and beauty are part of the floor upon which your brain sits. If you are feeling disconnected from those traits, if you are believing that it is not possible for human beings to agree upon them, turn inward, and illuminate this bone. It will fill you with soul-deep wisdom and help to heal your world.

On the inner edges of your eye sockets, near your tear glands, are two paired bones, small in size, known as the LACRIMALS. Small as they are, their function is ancient and important, for these are the Pillars of Justness bones. Not Justice, but *Justness*—a different quality, less about judgment than about harmony. When you tune into these bones near the eye, near the breath passages, your own sense of rightness, of justness, of harmony will be strengthened. These bones are not large, and that is part of their encoded meaning. To be just is not a huge thing, but a small one. And yet it is a vital thing as well. Often authority and might take the place of justness. They are loud and fierce and large. But in these tiny bones, all the justness you need will be found for all of humankind.

Within your ear are three tiny bones—the INCUS, MALLEUS, and STAPES—called the Guardian of Balance bones. Not shown in the chart, these tiny bones, when you tune into them, will help to keep you in spiritual balance. Sense them inwardly when you need to activate this quality of Self, of Soul; if they feel more clear in one side than the other, work with the *ooh* sound until you feel them equally, vibrating it into the weaker ear.

Your jawbone, known to physicians as the MANDIBLE, is known to us in the university as the Cup of Mindful Strength bone. Strength is not like power, whose energy and information are encoded in the pelvic bones. Power is about expression, and strength is an inner quality. And mindful strength is a quality needed by all as you work to create a life-enhancing global civilization. Think of the gesture of thoughtfulness—when you grasp your chin with one hand and rub it slowly. This is the gesture that helps to activate the energy and information stored in this bone. It is awakening mindful strength that will allow you to rebuild your world. Not brute, not wild, not unconscious, not vengeful, not fearful, but thoughtful strength, strength woven through with reason and vision, with hope and with caring, in this bone and in your lower teeth, which emerge from here—strength meeting wonderment when you chew.

There are two other bones found within your skull. They are called the NASAL CONCHA. Found within the nasal passages, these twin bones are called the Gates of Awe bones. As you inhale, breath passes over these bones and activates the capacity for awe. Awe is a pause in the body's movements. In your day and age, people have lost the capacity for awe. You seldom stand outdoors at night looking at the vast expanse of stars. You stand by the seashore, but the seas are so charted that they no longer hold mystery for you. The only pause left to you is fear. Your body still stops in fear. But awe is a benevolent and necessary pause. All sentient human beings must experience awe to be fully in alignment with All That Is. Becoming conscious of these tiny interior bones will activate this capacity in you—to stop, pause, and then become witness to the vast and endless miracle of physicality, of stardust and dancing and dreams.

The last bone of your head, the HYOID, is a tiny U-shaped bone found between your jaw and your throat. Floating in the midst of soft tissue, this curious singular bone, not shown on the chart, has the wonderful function of being the Anchor of Delight bone in all human bodies. Connected to your tongue, to the capacity to taste, taste being a doorway to delight, this little bone, when you tap into its patterned energy, allows you to be a transmitter/ receiver for joy in every cell. Up and down through your body, the hyoid will beam out this energy and draw it in. In times of pain, when you are feeling bored, lost, afraid, in need of comfort, draw your senses inward to this delicious little bone, and fill yourself with all the delight of beingness that has been encoded into it, into you, by your soul, which is you.

Although they may seem like bones, our TEETH actually develop from a different tissue layer than bones. Harder than bones, our mineral dense teeth are also encoded by the soul, and are the only encoded body parts we replace, losing our baby teeth so that our adult teeth can emerge. Both sets are known as the <u>Gates of Physicality</u>. The soul programs slightly different information in each set, appropriate to each stage of life. They are the guardians of our inner body and aid us in our connections with the physical world. The upper teeth emerge from the *maxilla,* and the lower from the *mandible,* and the two sets are further tuned with qualities associated with those bones. Like musical notes, each individual tooth also carries its own tone of physical wisdom. Click your teeth or rub them to activate their encoded wisdom.

The Bones of Your Legs

The PELVIS, or hipbones, form from three joined bones, the ilium, ischium, and pubis. They are known as the <u>Vessel of Power bones</u>. Here is the seat of strength, focus, and thrust in each incarnation. These paired bones, which connect with the sacrum, are the container for movement, drive, and achievement in your life. The gesture of placing hands on hips is an unconscious reminder of what is stored here, that you can deepen into when you do this gesture consciously, using sound and inner sight to access your encoded soul power.

The FEMURS, or upper leg bones, are the <u>Staff of Rightness bones</u>. Like a pair of inner compasses, these bones are directional devices, not for spatial direction but for right movement in your life. Feel and see these bones within you. They are large, and their heads are deep within your hip sockets. Feel the waves of energy that wash between them and know that when you access this information you will always be able to align yourself with your soul's right movement in this life.

The PATELLA, or kneecaps, are the Boundary Guardian bones. Just as the femurs tell you how to move, your kneecaps will tell you when to pause and how to pause. They are the first bones to move ahead of you into unknown space whenever you take a step. Tuning into them in stillness will allow you to become conscious of your own energetic boundaries. Being aware of them when you move will allow you to carry out that knowing into the world in all of your actions.

The TIBIA, or shinbones, are the Staff of Clarity bones. In a world of potential conflict and confusion, it is useful to have a place to go to for clarity, and that is the function of the tibiae. From before birth your soul has encoded these paired bones with information about your essential nature, your uniqueness as an individual that endures from lifetime to lifetime. And you can tap into this clarity by deepening into these bones. When you know this about yourself, you always have this knowledge to stand on, no matter what is going on around you. These are also the bones most likely to be bruised when you are moving around without clarity. When you are present and conscious in your tibiae, your life will be organized well.

The FIBULA are the bones of Spatial Knowing. These thinner companion bones to the tibiae have a related function. They have been encoded by your soul with information about the world and how to move in it. They are like radar devices and regulate how fast you move, whether you are comfortable in closed or open spaces, and offer guidance to you when you are moving through varied terrain. Hikers, bikers, tourists who read these bones will find their movement and journeys enhanced. Together with the information imprinted in the tibia, their information will allow you to move through the world safely.

There are seven ANKLEBONES, each with different names. Six of these bones have been imprinted with one set of information, and one with another. These six anklebones are known to us as the

Flexible Options bones. Tune into them when you are feeling uncertain, stuck, rigid. Flex and circle them to get this energy of motion moving in your body.

The CALCANEUS, or heel bones, are the bones of Planet Connection. This is apparent, for the heel is the bone that your body weight comes down on when you walk. Here are encoded all of your Earth contacts, everything you need to know about how to live on and with the planet. By holding this bone in your hand, the very firmness of the planet itself will be conveyed to you, and when you walk with your calcanei made conscious, you will walk as a proud child of Earth.

The long bones over the arch of your foot are called the META-TARSALS. There are five of them, which, together with the fourteen tiny bones in your toes called PHALANGES, are known to us in the Earth University as the Rods of Direction. By this we do not mean just physical direction, but also life direction. "Where am I going?" is a spiritual question just as it is a locational one. In the feet, your source of grounding, your soul has imprinted information on the direction of your life. In some traditions a spiritual guide is called a Director. In some traditions the washing of feet is a religious ritual. Wash your feet, rub them. Access the rich information contained there. For in truth, knowing the direction you want to go in is four-fifths of getting there, and these bones are your inner directors.

The Bones of Your Arms

The bone of the upper arm is called the HUMERUS. This long bone is called by us the Staff of Intention bone. Place your hand on this bone and deepen into it. In ancient times a clan ruler would hold the humerus bone of a worthy predecessor for guidance, and from this tradition comes the scepter of royalty.

When you tune into your own humerus bones, you make conscious connection with your own intentions. The humerus attaches to the scapula, the bone of dreams. It takes dreams and focuses them so that they can direct you as move in the world. When you walk, be aware of the way your arms swing, and see and feel your two humerus bones guiding you. Often, when thinking, you may find yourself holding your upper arm with your opposite hand or scratching your upper arm. At times of deep thought you may stand firm, with arms crossed over your chest so that you can grasp both upper arms. This is not an accidental gesture. It allows you to tap into the information there and tells others that you are clear in your intentions and someone to be reckoned with.

There are two swiveling bones in the lower arm, the *ulna* on the pinkie side and the *radius* on the thumb side. Each of these bones has a different but related function in its encodement. The two of them together are the source of creative soul information in your body. From intention to creativity, the arm bones are the tools that allow all human beings to reach out to the world in new and inventive ways. People instinctively rub their lower arms to get the creative juices flowing, and when you tune into them you can make conscious all the creativity of your immortal soul.

When you are standing with your arms hanging at your side, your ULNA is behind you. It is the <u>bone of Creative Measure</u>. Creativity has its own seasons, and these must be followed, ridden like a self-directed wave. Seasons of work always follow seasons of rest and new gestation. In cultures that view creativity as a job rather than a process, the natural creative rhythms will be overridden. Tuning into this bone will reconnect you with your own interior creative cycles.

The RADIUS, the bone in front when you stand with your arms hanging at your side, is the <u>bone of Creative Expression</u>, encoded by your soul with all the information you will need to fully express yourself in this lifetime. Hold this bone and deepen into it. Sitting above your thumb, it is the miracle of your ancestors' creativity, for it allows you to hold and grasp objects and interact with your physical world in far different ways than those in which animals with paws can. And it is in and through the radius that your creativity can be met and made conscious. Every human being alive is an artist of one kind or another—a cook, a storyteller, a musician, a dancer, a healer, a friend, a peacekeeper. And the wisdom of your own art is carried in this bone.

There are eight small bones in the wrist, called CARPALS. All of them are programmed with the same information. These bones are the Seat of Creative Modulation bones. Just as creativity has seasons, it must also have limits. Not limits in time, but limits in conception. There is an expression that is embodied in the wrist bones: "Don't let your reach exceed your grasp." These are the bones that modulate creative energy—that, when you pay attention to them, tell you where your limits are. Often people end up with something you call carpal tunnel syndrome, because they have overridden the information these bones are programmed to give you. Frequently, under stress, people rub their wrists, trying to rub out the tension there. If they will listen to those bones instead, they will not undertake activities beyond their natural focus.

There are five METACARPAL bones in the palm of the hand and fourteen PHALANGES in the fingers. Taken together, these nineteen bones are known as the River of Expression bones. Stroke them, rub them, and feel the information they carry, for part of expression is receptive, and it is through these wonderful bones that you can read your other bones as well, so as to more fully manifest yourself in the world. For each of these bones has been imprinted by your soul with wisdom concerning your capacity for expression. When you rub your hands and palms in times of stress, you are unconsciously activating these bones. Each one of them contains soul information that can answer the pressing question "What now?" When you shake out your hands, you are discarding the energy of old choices so that you can choose new directions. And these bones know all your options in terms of expression. The fingers have language and music and meaning in them. Each one is another brilliant instrument of your unfolding. As you get to know your fingers, you will know where to turn for inspiration. These bones are the voice of the inner muse of your own immortal soul.

How to Be Present as Your Bones and as Your Entire Body

You may think of a skeleton as the symbol of death, but in fact your bones are the source of life in you, and as you sit and read these words, your skeleton is fully present in you.

Feel your bones; fill them with blue light and with vibration. Spend time each day, as you wake and as you fall into sleep, learning to see and feel your bones, your skeleton, from the inside, on the inside. As you move, as you walk, all through the day, see and hear and feel your bones inside you. Tune into them all, and know that you are richly encoded by your soul, by your Self, with all the information you need to move through life, fully present, fully alive, fully aware, fully conscious, fully sentient.

Rejoice in your bones! They are not static, they are not finished. Although they are the symbol of death, these bones of yours are the doorway to life and to wisdom. And not only are they encoded by your soul, but, like hologram bits, each and every bone in your body is storing energy and information from every single moment of your life, sleeping and waking. In life as they will be in death, your bones are a living record of your beingness. The Biblical prophet Ezekiel had a vision of a valley of dry bones all coming to life again. When we tune into our bones, they will be a source of constant renewal for us. And should someone a thousand years from now pick up any one of your bones and know what is encoded there, he or she would be able to read the tone and feeling, the learning and the wisdom you brought with you and accumulated throughout your life.

Bones are the vessels of soul in the world of form. So hard, so dense, these inner crystals are waiting inside to enlighten you at every moment. They are the matrix around which your body assembles itself, and they continue throughout your life to feed the other rivers of information that live within you. You have been taught to think of your brain and your nerves as two separate parts of one system, your brain the seat of consciousness in your head, supplying information to and supplied information by the nerves in your body. But in truth they are inseparable, and this river of consciousness that courses through your entire body is something that you can learn to connect with as a single unit. Feel yellow light pouring into this river in your body, enlivening it from head to toe. Use a high-pitched tone of *eee*. Feel and see the way that your nervous system weaves together bone-deep wisdom into the present, into the world of incarnation—connects all of your rich history to the world and allows you to move in it in a conscious way. This the primary physical information system, evolving from the very earliest living organisms into the brilliant form you find within you.

There is another river in your body, and one more simple to think of in that flowing form: your circulation system. Feel it now in your body, glowing red-bright and alive. Feel your heart, arteries, veins, capillaries, and all the other liquid-bearing channels inside you. Turn your senses deeper inward and feel all the blood and other body fluids in every part of you—a single constantly moving river. Use the sound *ah* to activate this turning inward. Fed by your bones from within, your heart and circulation system carry wisdom that is not personal in the way the wisdom of your bones is. This is the very wisdom of the beating heart of the planet. In your blood, lymph, cerebro-spinal, joint, and extracellular fluids are carried all of life's history on your world, from its first beginnings in water. When you deepen into and connect with your body's liquid, beating consciousness, you are swimming in the very river of life itself.

Your internal organs and glands produce a different tone in the symphony of who you are now, rising up like the rest of your body and full of your ancestral history. Fill them with a deep green light and be present with them. Work with the sound *ooh*. Feel the way they are sheltered and supported by your bones, fed and connected by blood and nerves, giving voice to the diversity of life on Earth. The organs of your digestive tract are the expression of the capacity to assimilate what is needed and discard what is nonessential—and on every level. Your liver is the moist soil of Earth with its genius for transformation, your lungs the essence of the trees. Your urinary tract and its organs are the purification of form. Your glands are internal monitors and regulators. When you enter into all these systems, you deepen your capacity for living as a body.

Your muscles, tendons, ligaments, fascia, and skin are another river of consciousness. Filled with a rich pink light, they can become known to you. Use the sound *aa*. Like the nerves within you, they are a mediating system—between you and the world of time, space, and motion. They carry within them the wisdom of movement, change, and connection. They are the outer face of your bones, the part of you that touches the world.

So too the inner channels of the meridians known to the ancients of the East are a part of your body. Feel them circulating a soft silver light. Use a high-pitched tone *ai*. These fine vessels are the doorway between the subtle and the physical bodies, and are the monitors of your energy from before you are born until death.

Be whole in your body, alive in every part of it. Be like the Earth, each river flowing through the caverns and mountains of your bones, with no separation between any of these different rivers. For this is who you are right now, this unity. This is who you are right now, immortal soul embodied. And the more present you are in your body, the more you fulfill your destiny as a soul, the more you are able to participate in the creation of heaven on Earth. Bones the armature. Body the vehicle. You the creator. For all the world, a blessing.

Chapter 7

THE AWAKENING OF THE SUBTLE BODY

As we become conscious in our physical bodies, we can actively participate in their evolution. This evolution is not separate from the global transformation we are working toward. In addition to our physical bodies, we are also the creators and possessors of a subtle body, composed of organs and vessels of a very different kind. Even the matter the subtle body is made of is different from the atomic matter that we are familiar with. The particles of this matter are different and obey different rules than do the subatomic particles our scientists have discovered in the twentieth century.

The subtle body is the mediator between our souls and our physical bodies. It is through the subtle body that our souls encode our bones. In fact, we possess two non-physical bodies, one less dense than the other, that coexist with our physical form and survive us after death. In the material that follows we will be exploring those two bodies, with information from Arrasu, Tabbad, and my companion angel Sargolais on aspects that are vital to our evolution at this time.

✴   ✴   ✴

Sentience, as we saints and angels call it, is an interface of physical and energetic consciousness. On the Planet Earth it is the possession of two different peoples: the human beings and the cetacean beings. In the realm of total consciousness, each people embodies the capacity to receive different frequency bands in the range of cosmic consciousness.

Everything that is has consciousness, although we use that word in a different way than you do. To us not only animals, plants, and even bacteria and viruses have consciousness, but so too do rocks, sand, dust, atoms, and subatomic particles. As consciousness accretes in the world of energy and matter, it becomes capable of receiving and transmitting patterns of energy that we call information. Creatures with such consciousness function at a level of beingness we angels call awareness, the quality of self that is possessed by animals. When awareness continues to accrete around consciousness, like pearl around a grain of sand, what we angels call sentience appears.

Sentience has several different attributes; self-awareness is one of them, and it manifests due to the evolution of certain organs in the subtle body, the interfaces between the physical and energetic aspects just spoken of. These organs, the chakras, appear in other animals, but there are fewer of them than in cetaceans and in humans. Just as a computer with more chips can function at a more complex level, a life-form with more of these organs will be able to function at a more complex level also.

A species such as your own attained sentience when the crown chakra awakened and its awareness system evolved from six to seven chakras. For thousands of years, shamans, mystics, and healers on every part of the planet have been aware of the chakras, studied them, explored them, and worked with them in healing. Many of you are familiar with them and with the river of self that they create in your bodies.

The root or base chakra at the tip of the spine focuses the energies of security, survival, and groundedness to the Earth.

The sexual or abdominal chakra, found about two inches below the navel, is concerned with sexuality, fertility, and creativity.

The solar plexus chakra is in the upper abdomen. Its function is of will, drive, focus, and direction.

The heart chakra can be found in the middle of the chest at heart level. It is the center for love and intimacy.

The throat chakra, found at the base of the neck, is the energetic center for communication.

The third eye or brow chakra, located in the middle of the forehead, is the seat of intuition and psychic abilities.

The crown chakra, at the top of the head, is the source of cosmic consciousness and God connection.

Now, in your own time, a new major chakra is beginning to awaken. The seed of this new chakra has always been present in the human body, waiting for the right moment in history to be activated. As this organ awakens in all of you, your entire species will be united energetically for the first time, and you will be ready to begin a journey toward higher levels of perception.

This new chakra is found in the mid-chest area, between the heart and throat chakras. It is called by many different names, including the thymus chakra and the high heart, secret heart, or witness area. You can locate it two fingers' width below the notch in your clavicle, right where your second set of ribs sticks out.

The function of the heart chakra is to generate personal love, compassion, and intimacy. The function of the high heart or thymus chakra is to generate, transmit, and receive the energies of peace, joy, and global connection. This new chakra is part of an energetic web that will eventually link everyone on the planet.

It takes three to five years to fully activate the thymus chakra. Turn inward and feel a tiny aqua flame burning in your upper chest. Feel this blue-green fire growing stronger. Vibrate sound into this chakra. Feel the way that it beams out energy to the thymus area of people around you. Feel the way in which it is connected energetically to everyone else who has awakened this chakra.

New disorders of the immune system, of which the thymus gland is a major organ, are raising your awareness of this area of your bodies. As you awaken your thymus chakras, the thymus gland will be energized and strengthened. This will help you deal with increasing stresses on your immune systems due to heightening environmental imbalances during this time of radical transformation on the planet.

This eighth chakra is awakening now because you have evolved to the point where you are ready to live in peace, harmony, and global cooperation. In fact, the external changes you are trying to make in the world are dependent upon all of humanity's awakening their thymus chakras. For when this chakra is awakened in everyone, you will know in your bodies that all of humanity is connected and that all of us, incarnate and discarnate, are members of one sentient species, sharing a common destiny and a common world.

The evolution of humanity is not separate from the evolution of your chakras. Up until now it has taken seven to be sentient. As you move on to eight and beyond, new options are available to you, options that may allow your species to diversify as the cetaceans have. You are moving toward a time when, rather than seven or eight chakras, more than twelve chakras will be able to function in human bodies. Like automobiles, which come with standard features and available options, the eight human chakras will be standard, and the additional chakras will be optional. Some of you may decide to awaken all of them, others none, still others a few. A short description of the major new chakras follows.

The mid-abdominal chakra is located between the navel and the solar plexus. The function of this chakra is to integrate and activate Earth-focused wisdom. This chakra will be the seat in you of the planetary will. Humans who activate it will move through the world as group facilitators, tuned in their cells to the thoughts and needs of the planet. This chakra, a bridge between the creativity and fertility of the sexual chakra and the self-directed will of the individual, will modulate will in such a fashion that war and competition will not be possible among humans. Those who awaken this chakra will be energetic guides to movement, rather like the birds who fly at the front of a formation. They are not the rulers of the flock but the guides in movement of its collective

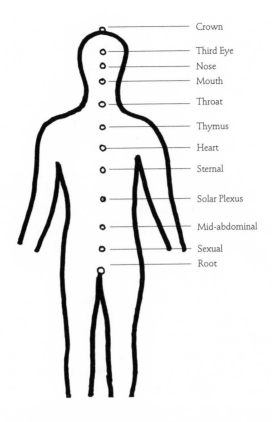

Crown

Third Eye

Nose

Mouth

Throat

Thymus

Heart

Sternal

Solar Plexus

Mid-abdominal

Sexual

Root

will. This center of wisdom, when awakened, will be that which distinguishes your leaders from those of the past. In the future, whoever leads will be organically following the will of the planet that birthed you.

The seed of the next major chakra can be found in the space between the solar plexus and heart chakras. We will call this chakra the sternal chakra. When it is awakened in an individual, he or she will be attuned to the energies of tenderness and caring at levels deeper than humanity has known until this time. And this capacity for tenderness will be nongendered, and of a different strand of connection than that of the sexual chakra or the heart chakra or the thymus. The energy of this organ is nurturant in a way that sees the unfolding patterns of those it reaches out to. It is not hierarchical, it is not a parenting energy. Nor is it a lover energy. It is the emergent seat of caring in action, the expressive mode of what you have at times called compassion. Those who awaken it will be found among dancers, athletes, manual laborers, and others who are deeply focused in the physical.

It may seem that something we will call the mouth chakra should be a vehicle of communication. However, the function of this potential organ of wisdom in the human body is other than that. The tongue is a sensory device, the source of taste and temperature and texture. The evolving mouth chakra will have similar capacities, on an energetic level. This new chakra will allow human beings who activate it to receive and transmit information about energetic patterns like weather, and emotional patterns that might be called emotional weather. You make use of this sense in certain ways already when you feel the energy in a room or sense it in someone else. But this kind of sensing will deepen and be fully embodied through this chakra. Those of you who choose to activate it will be community pattern sensers, pattern tasters. This chakra will enable you to experience and communicate about levels of behavior that are now unconscious.

The final major awakening chakra is the nose chakra. As soon as you say those words—*nose chakra*—you may find yourself smiling or laughing. The nose is a humorous organ in most human cultures, and the chakra connected with the nose will carry that light and happy energy with it. "Follow your nose," you say in your English language, as an animal might follow its senses. This chakra is one that was formerly awakened in human beings, but your species chose to deactivate it as the ice ages came to a close, so that you could develop the third eye and other areas of awareness. In reawakening this chakra you will be tapping into deep levels of perception that are now unconscious, and you will do so in ways that are easy, delightful, and pleasurable for all.

After reading this catalog of newly awakening chakras, give yourselves time to turn inward and explore your own body. Notice the places within where you find flickerings of energy that correspond to these new centers. Sit quietly and turn your senses inward so that you can be with and explore the energies and information that will come to you as you awaken them. The future evolution of humanity is tied to their awakening. Each of you, alone, with others, as you tune into these new chakras, adds to the sentience capacities of the entire human species, and further to your collective unfolding into harmony and peace and planetary transformation. Those of you who began your cycles of incarnation on this world will find these chakras within yourselves. Those of you who have lived on other worlds may find within yourselves additional chakras with even more unusual capacities. Celebrate this unfolding. It is the doorway to the future, alive and glowing within you all.

Beyond the subtle body that contains the chakras and the myriad vessels that connect them to each other and the meridians of the physical body, there is a second nonphysical body that all of you possess, even more subtle, even less physically focused. This body has different organs than the chakra body does that are not easy to feel at your current level of consciousness. Its endless fibers weave their way into all the chakras and the vessels of that subtle body. There is, however, one distinguishing feature of this *subtle* subtle body—a feature you can open yourselves up to at this time, that will help you to become more conscious of this level of your greater self.

Turn inward and feel a tracery of golden light in your body. Feel it weaving through every part of you, shimmering, finer than silk, finer than the delicate webs of spiders—and strong enough to last for eons. These golden fibers sparkle within your physical body, circulating within it. But there is one set of fibers that is capable of extending out beyond your body. The seeds of these fibers can be found curled up on either side of your spine, in the spaces between each vertebra. Bring your consciousness there. Feel that you can breathe life and energy and warmth into those golden seeds, so that the fibers awaken, uncurl, and begin to expand outward, exactly like wings, out beyond your back and fluttering, out to more than three feet. See the drawing on the next page for the location of the seed-sites and awakened fibers.

This winged body is the interface between your soul in its spaceless/timeless dimension and the subtle body in its realm of fluid space/time. So too the subtle body with its chakras is the interface between your winged body and your physical body, alive and conscious in the world of linear space/time that you know as

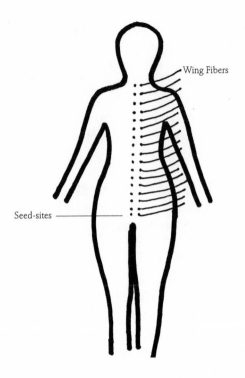

Wing Fibers

Seed-sites

the universe. Feel with all your inner and outer senses the coexisting layers of this fourfold you:

soul

winged body

subtle body

physical body

This four-layered being is you in all of your fullness, all of your aliveness—an ocean of consciousness flowing between mortal and immortal shores, between time and timeless moments, between beaches of space and infinite horizons. And all of this, you are. All of this is you, as vast as the universe, and waiting to be charted. When you, like an astronaut who turns outward to the stars, when you turn inward to the layers of who you are, you make possible God's dream for sentient beings, God's rich dream for human life upon this world.

Revelations for a New Millennium

Chapter 8

A JOURNEY OF TRANSFORMATION

 There are many ways to heal, many ways to change
and grow—religious and philosophical, collective and
personal. More than any other nondenominational organization, the Twelve Step community has changed the
way we live in the world. You may not consider yourself
a part of this community, but from its founding in 1935,
Alcoholics Anonymous and the groups that emerged from
it—Al-Anon, OA, NA, ACOA, and so forth—without
dues, government funding, or elected officials, have been
a source of comfort, healing, hope, and renewal for their
members, and have brought to public awareness matters
previously not talked about, matters ranging from sub-
stance abuse to emotional, physical, and sexual abuse.

Many of us know that AA was founded by two alcoholics, Bill W. and Dr. Bob. Few, however, know of the
contribution of a Being of Light that appeared to Bill W.
while he was close to death in a drying-out hospital, a
being that helped him turn his life around. So, behind the
workings of AA and its offspring, the angels have also
been at work as silent partners. The founders of AA were
careful about how they spoke of God and about their
mystical experiences. Today it is easier for us to talk about

our spirituality. *Whole bookstores and university programs now exist that offer spiritual guidance. As the world has changed, so too have changed the patterns of healing that we can use, changed and grown from the first steps created by the founders of AA.*

In the section that follows, dictated to me by Arrasu and Sargolais, you will find information on personal transformation for the coming era, focused around ten steps that we can all take on our journeys. These steps do not replace the familiar steps of AA, but are for anyone on a spiritual journey. You may not think of yourself as someone in need of recovery, but when we look around at the world we have created—at the wars, crime, drugs, pollution—it is easy to see that all of us are in need of healing from the excesses, the abuses, and the limitations of a dying civilization. What follows is one path, one of many.

※　　※　　※

Remembering Your Power

Once there was a time when people honored everyone who was born into their families and into their tribes. All women were honored for their wisdom, and all men were honored. Blind people were honored and so were deaf people—for their own special gifts, different from everyone else's, that added to the life and richness of the tribe. People that we would call handicapped or disabled, mentally and physically, were honored and cherished for the tenderness, the special wisdom, and the compassion that they brought with them. Men who love men were honored for their special powers, as were women who love women. So there were lineages, for example, of deaf and lesbian elders, who knew their own wisdom and were able to teach the young of the next generation how to deepen into theirs, for the fulfillment of their own lives and for the good of all the people.

Once there was a time when people honored everyone who was born into their families, born into their tribes. This was a long time ago, at the end of the last Ice Age, before we as a species chose the path we find ourselves on now, one of separation and differentiation. We as a species chose this path to further our own evolution; but although we have grown from it, much of it has been a journey into pain and fear. We are coming to the end of this journey. We are making new choices as a species. We are coming into a time when we will learn from love and not from fear, from joy and not from pain. We are creating this new time of wholeness together.

In those days, everyone was honored for who they were. They were recognized from early childhood, their gifts were recognized from early childhood, and from early childhood they were taught by the seers and healers and shamans that were older than they. They were recognized, and they were taught to use their gifts and powers for all the people. And we are coming to a time when the world will be this way again, when everyone's gifts will be recognized, guided, and honored. Knowledge of this ancient time is built into our genetic structures. The expectations of that ancient time are encoded into all our bodies. And you too can connect with them in yourself. So give yourself time to read these words, in a place where you will not be disturbed. Let the words sink deep into your body and your consciousness.

As a pilgrim on a journey of healing and transformation, know and believe that in the old days your innate gifts would have been recognized, in the days before this cycle of history began. Know that you would have been loved in childhood for your essential nature, and taught by your elders how to deepen into your own special powers and wisdom.

Know this and remember this. Feel it. And feel the pain and sorrow that you carry—for as a child in this life no one recognized you, no one saw your beauty and your gifts, no one taught you how to use them, although you announced yourself as best you could and waited for your teachers to appear.

Breathe in these words and know that you can release your pain and sorrow. There were no elders in your childhood, there was no one there to teach you how to be who you are. But the time will come again when children will be honored and recognized. And because of the journey you took, you are one of the people who will help to create this time for future generations.

Feel the pain you still carry inside. Know that you can release it. You can release guilt, release fear, release anger, release shame, release blame, release doubt. Feel them in your body, feel their shape and size, their texture, and the places you hold them in. Then, breathe them out with each exhalation. Your journey to wholeness is one that you create for yourself. It will take as long as it takes. But you can work with your body to release the old burdens you are still carrying in each and every breath you take.

Now, go deep inside yourself, beneath all of your old pain and fear. Go deep into your heart, into your dreams. Feel your visions, feel your gifts. Feel all the places inside you where you carry your own ancient wisdom. Feel the places where you carry them in your mind and in your body. Each time you inhale, breathe in the golden light of your winged body, to warm and enliven those places where your dreams live so that they expand out into every part of you, till they flow through you and fill up every cell.

In the past there were elders and teachers. But in this time, at the end of a century and the beginning of a new millennium, so many of us came into the world alone, began our journeys alone. We did this to test ourselves, to temper our souls as they manifested in the world of form. Danger after danger we moved through, and here we are today, healing and becoming whole, whole and standing in our power again, as a gift to all the world, and as guides for everyone who follows us to learn and grow from. Stop for a moment and know that everything you did was a part of your emergence into power. Feel the ancient gifts you carry deep within your cells. Breathe into who you are, and stand proudly. You have tested your strength on a soul level—and you have passed the test.

Our Shared Dreams

Through our collective suffering as a species we have become wise. Through our collective sorrow as a species we have developed great compassion. Through our collective evils as a species we have become loving. Everything we have done as a species we chose to do on a soul level. We have all lived lives in different times and places. Each of us has been red, yellow, black, and white, female and male, slave and master, wise and foolish, straight and gay. The soul is genderless, stateless, and raceless. It is the collective of world souls in the Earth University that has shaped our evolution as a species. And together we have learned from our evils, learned from our wounds, just as a child learns who puts a hand in fire, learns not to do it again, learns to honor fire. So we are wise and compassionate and loving and strong. We are making new choices as a species. And who you are is a part of our transformation. The path you walk is a part of our healing.

In the journey to joy, we will come to understand that every experience in our lives is a teacher, and that nothing we do is a mistake. We can learn from everything. And in doing so, we make possible a world where we will not have to learn from pain, because we have taken from it all that it can teach. In that future world, all children will be recognized in childhood. They will not need to walk alone. Elders like you will be there to nurture and support them, to teach them to trust their visions and to learn how to use them for everyone. For, like any muscles, vision muscles must be trained and exercised. And when they are, they will carry us far into the future.

Feel your strength. Go back into your childhood and allow yourself to remember your earliest dreams, your first visions. Allow yourself to remember how sensitive you are, how open you are. And now honor all of these as your gifts, as part of your strength, as the outflowing of your personal power.

Look deeply into yourself and know that you came into this life to make a difference in your family, you came into this life to make a difference in this world. No one was there to teach you how to use your visions and your powers. Perhaps you were frightened by them. Perhaps your family was frightened by them. No one was there to hold and nurture the vision-child you were. Feel your inner child, and hold it in the lap of your wise and loving inner elder. Let yourself become your inner child's best teacher. Be there for yourself. Love that inner child exactly as it is—wounded, wise, and healing. Know that in this time you have been your own guide, your own teacher, and done the best you could to cultivate your gifts.

Honor the seed of who you are. Honor the journey that you can go on when you accept the truth about who you are, and stop living in the falsehoods you were told or told yourself in order to try to make sense of who you are. Remember your dreams and record them, in words and in pictures. Remember your dreams, for they belong to everyone; remember both the dreams you have at night and the dreams you dream by day.

Parents used to think that babies were like lumps of clay, waiting to be shaped and molded. But we come into this world as ourselves. We do not need to be molded; we need to be supported and guided to trust who we are, who we were born to be. And your journey to recovery will make a new world possible. For just as your dreams belong to everyone, the healing work you have done you did for everyone, too. For you are Everyperson. And when you honor this, and when you honor your inner nature, you can walk the stars—without ever taking your feet off the ground.

Ten Steps to Transformation

The ancient sage and Earth University adviser Lao-tzu said that the journey of a thousand miles begins with the first step. Just by turning your body and facing in a new direction, wherever you find yourself, you can begin a new journey, take a step in a new direction. In times past we angels gave you twelve steps to work with in your journey to healing. They are but twelve steps of many in the journey to self. The Ten Steps we present here are designed to carry you to another part of the forest of consciousness. For some of you they will build upon the familiar Twelve Steps. For others they will be a new exploration. Either way, as you walk them they will take you to a land beyond duality, beyond higher and lower powers, to a place where there is one power only— love—a spark of which shines out from every heart.

Step One

Know in your bones, your heart, your body, and your mind that you are powerful and capable of managing your life, in harmony with your soul, with God, and together with the members of your chosen communities.

Keep a journal so that you can record the steps of your journey and go back to see where you have been. Notice the changes you have made in your life. Honor those changes. Celebrate them. Begin each day by taking time to feel that you are a being of love, that you are growing and changing and aligning yourself more and more with the essence of love that permeates the universe.

Step Two

As you travel your spiritual path, recognize that everything you did was a part of your journey to Spirit, chosen at the deepest level, and a part of your soul's unfolding.

Could you be who you are without the journey you have been on, without the darkness, the horrors, the fear? Know that you have created this journey on a soul level so that you could learn all you needed to in order to become more fully yourself. Feel all your feelings, and ask yourself how each event in your life, however painful, was the perfect teacher for you to learn exactly what you needed to learn at that time.

Step Three

Remember that each moment is a new creation, with something new to teach. And you are ready to learn from joy now, in each moment. Take it in tiny sips, letting it transmute your body until you are filled with joy and overflowing. Then you can make choices in clear, heart-centered, deeply grounded ways, and then each moment of your life will be another opportunity for celebration.

Each meal can be a joyous feast, each gathering with friends can be a festival. Beneath your pain, the miracle of life is waiting to be felt. Learn to do loving things for yourself every day, things that do not cost money, that nurture you without your having to put anything in your body. Celebrate flowers and birds and clouds and sun and wind and rain. Songs, dances, poems, prayers, laughter, silence, sharing—these are some of the appropriate ways to express gratitude and thanksgiving and soul-vast celebration. We have learned from suffering for so long that our bodies are not used to joy. But each day we can take in more and more of it, transmuting our cells till they are filled with it.

Step Four

In addition to releasing pain and healing your wounds by talking about them with friends, in therapy, or in recovery groups, you may want to start doing body work—be it massage, movement, breath work, herbal treatment, in whatever modality feels safe—with wise and grounded facilitators, to discover and let go of any blocks and traumas that remain in your physical and in your subtle bodies.

Begin each day by massaging yourself, by feeling your breath. Visualize roots emerging from the bottom of your spine and the bottoms of your feet, connecting you to the Earth at all times, to ground you in your body and in your day-to-day life. You are a soul who has chosen to experience physicality. Use the healing wisdom of others to support you in being grounded and present, knowing that they are there to support you in your own healing, in connecting you with your own capacity to heal yourself.

Step Five

You are more than just your present mind and body, and you may decide to explore your past lives and the information you carry on a soul level, and begin to do the work necessary for you to own and make use of that wisdom in your daily life.

Notice the clues to your past, the curious likes and dislikes that seem to have nothing to do with your upbringing or history. Feel the part of you that has always known that you are more than just who you are now. Go on this journey slowly and in the way that will be most loving for who you are right now. You do not have to force it. Open to it and let it teach you. Others will be there to support you—books and teachers and healers and friends both new and old. Memories may come to you in dreams or visions as well.

Step Six

Find the people who added to your life and express to them your gratitude for having been there when you needed their wisdom, love, tenderness, and strength. Honor the part of yourself that has been there for others, too, and allow yourself to take in their gratitude if they express it to you.

Each of you carries love and wisdom for everyone. A smile at the right moment can be a deep healing. And so often you forget to thank those around you for their gifts. A letter burned can be a spiritual thank-you to those who have died or whom you cannot find. A call or letter from the heart is a thank-you. Cultivate gratitude in the garden of your heart. And learn to receive it also, when it is given.

Step Seven

All of humanity is connected from body to body in an energetic network. Awaken your thymus chakra so that you can feel your connection to all of humanity, and step out into the world each day in a soul-connected way.

The thymus chakra is the pearl of great price that you have all been searching for. When it is awakened in all of you, you will never feel alone again. Connected in an energetic web, you will become the collective messiah you have all been waiting for, anointed with divine light just above your hearts. For all of you come into the world with wisdom, and all of your wisdom is needed to heal the world. You come into the world like snowflakes, each of you unique, each of you sparkling.

Step Eight

You share this world with many beings, in and out of physical bodies. Open yourself to all who live here, for guidance and in community, and open yourself to the guidance of the saints and angels as well. You are never alone. The universe is ever waiting to reveal itself to you.

Animal and plant guides are always with you. Ancestors, saints, and angels are with you too. As you open to your greater beingness, you can feel and hear and speak to them more and more consciously, you can begin to co-create with them on deeper and deeper levels. For so long humans have acted against the world instead of with it. By opening to all of life, you will learn to move in alignment with every other life-form and with the planet itself. You will learn to find comfort in connection and not possessions, in dance and not destruction.

Step Nine

You have never been separate from God. Its love and bliss are the ground of all being, the source of the true nature you were born to express in the world. Through prayer and meditation you will experience this yourself. Each day proudly thank God in your own ways for having created you, a child of the universe.

Celebration leads to gratitude, and gratitude leads to joy, union, reunion. Find ways that help you to experience the Oneness of All That Is. Feel it in yourself and in the universe. Know that a twig is as much a part of the Oneness as a star is. Let this be your spiritual practice, to feel God in everything, and to feel the Oneness in yourself, too.

Step Ten

Share your beauty, love, wisdom, joy, and connectedness with all of humanity, with all who live on this planet, with the planet itself, with the Universe, and with God, in each word and thought of your waking and sleeping life. Let your joy ripple out into the world in concrete actions each day, in ways that feel appropriate to you, that will help to create heaven on Earth.

You are all on a journey of transformation. Everyone who is alive now is a part of this journey. Each of you has a different role to play. When you acknowledge the Divine in everyone and in everything, you support the transformation. Let yourself feel the life that pulses in Father/Mother Earth. Know that who you are and what you do and how you grow into joy are part of the unfolding of the Creator's dreams and visions. Celebrate. Share your joy. For many think that a spiritual journey is a passive and solitary thing. But a spiritual journey is something that happens in community, and it is something to be expressed not just in thoughts and prayers, but, ultimately, in all of your actions.

Creating Heaven on Earth

If you have been on a spiritual journey, you know from your own experience that it is possible to change your life. In community you have experienced others doing the same heroic work. If you are in a prayer or meditation group, if you are in therapy or in recovery, you are already part of the movement for change that is sweeping our planet. And now it is time for you to own your inner gifts and take part in the shared journey of global transformation. In exploring these Ten Steps, you can deepen your commitment to healing. "God does not want us to be perfect," we angels say to you. "It wants us to be present." This is true for saints and cetaceans, for angels, and for humans. As you own your gifts, you will become more and more present—in your body, in your life, and in the world.

Imagine a world where everyone is consciously healing, from abuse and from fear, from ageism, racism, sexism, and homophobia, in recovery from ethnic, regional, and religious conflict, and, at the core of it, in recovery from feeling separate from our Creator.

Once there was a time when shamans and seers and visionaries and world-dreamers were honored by all the people. They were taught how to use their gifts for themselves and for all of humanity, in harmony with the planet and the cosmos. If you are on a spiritual journey, you carry within yourself the seeds of transformation that all the Earth is in need of right now. The air, water, and soil you depend on are in need of healing. Scientists and politicians do not have the cure. But you who have already transmuted your life have access to the inner love, inner wisdom, inner power to do remarkable things. Own your power. Own your visions. Own your gifts. Together, we can create a heaven on Earth. Together, we can create the world we know is possible. Together, we can all live out our deepest dreams, in harmony with all of life, and in harmony with the dream of our Creator—the dream that gave birth to us all.

Chapter 9

BEGINNING STEPS
IN CONSCIOUS DYING

We cannot talk about our rich history, about the gifts of physicality or the wisdom embodied in our bones, without also talking about another aspect of human life—death.

This chapter could have been called "The Doorway to Re-dying," for if we have lived lifetime after lifetime, then we have all also died before, again and again. For much of human history, life expectancy was brief. Young men died in wars, young women died in childbirth, and infant and child mortality rates were high. Each brief life and death was another opportunity for a soul to touch into physicality, taste it, learn from it, then die again, reorganize, absorb that information and work with it in the disembodied Earth University, and then come back again.

There are still places on this planet where life expectancy is short, but in other regions people in greater and greater numbers are living longer and longer lives. Instead of having to die physically to reorganize, we are all learning how to die and be reborn in the same physical life. These many small deaths, and the constant minor death we experience every single night of our lives, when our minds are free to roam the universe with our souls—all of them allow us to practice what I call re-dying, so that we can master the big death when it comes.

Death is a part of life. The angels compare it to a great painter signing with a flourish her signature on the bottom of a canvas she has just finished. Every journey into a body needs that same kind of completion. But we have come to fear death, to see death as the enemy of life rather than its culmination. In the section that follows, from Tabbad and Arrasu, you will have an opportunity to look at death and re-death in a different way. When you allow yourself to remember that you have not only lived before but died before, you can bring to the one inevitable event of life that all of us will share a consciousness and clarity that will allow you to return to the Earth University and your friends and teachers there not with sorrow and a sense of loss and failure, but with joy and satisfaction and a soul-deep feeling of completion. Then death is not something to fear, to say no to, but rather the ultimate orgasm of life, the fullest possible yes that any one of us can say.

✻   ✻   ✻

All of you will die. All of you are midwives for the dying. Death is something you fear. You no longer live in an age when birth is as deadly as it used to be. But until very recently, and still today in many parts of the world, both infant and mothers' mortality rates were high. Birth and death touch closely. Today, it is largely the pain that is feared. But birth is like putting the Atlantic Ocean in a soda bottle, and death is like breaking the bottle. Which one do you think is more difficult?

In the journey to being fully embodied, you cannot avoid talking about death. Your soul is immortal, but your body isn't. If you are on a spiritual path, it is easy to say, "Why should I cry? Mom is still alive somewhere." This is true, but it is not all the truth. For you knew your mother as a body, and bodies feel the loss of other bodies. You cannot escape feeling grief by focusing only on her journeying elsewhere.

When you know about dying, it is easier to stop fearing it. When you are fully alive in your body, you do not need to create illness or pain in order to get out of it. When you know that you are capable of consciously dying, you can leave an incarnation in a very different way.

Death is the slipping away of the subtle bodies and the soul from the physical body. You may engage in it slowly—so slowly over time that there is almost no single moment when you go from being alive to being dead. Or you may die in an instant, by accident or by design. On a soul level, all death is chosen. This may not, however, be your conscious experience in your physical body, or in your subtle bodies, either, but it is known by the soul, chosen by the soul, always.

Once people knew how to die consciously. Animals still know how to do this. They go off by themselves and unwind when their time has come. But in order to progress mentally, humanity long ago made the choice to step away from many kinds of instinctual behavior, and one of the many skills that was "lost" to most of you was conscious dying.

The subtle bodies are composed of a different kind of matter than the physical body, are not subject to the same rules of space/time existence as your physical body. They exist in a different kind of space, nonlinear, just as they exist in a very fluid realm of time. They do not have to get from here to there by going through all the points in between. And they do not have to get from now to then by going through the days in between. Before you are born your soul weaves together your physical body and your subtle bodies by "slowing down" so that it can work with the laws of three-dimensional reality.

Babies cry whenever they find themselves "stuck" in matter. It takes time to get used to it. In dreams, however, your souls may drift away for a time, just as they do in certain kinds of altered states of consciousness, leaving only tendril fibers to connect them until they return.

If you think of the soul as a driver, the subtle bodies as clothing, and the physical body as a car, then you can think of birth as the way that you put on your seat belt, anchoring your Self into the vehicle. Dying is taking off your seat belt and slipping out of the automobile. But you are "belted in" in every chakra, major and minor. So you have to unbelt yourself from each one, too.

In the days when people still knew how to do this, there were chants they would recite for someone who wanted to die or who was dying. They were like your song "The foot bone's connected to the anklebone; the anklebone's connected to the leg bone." Starting at the bottom, they would work their way up, from chakra to chakra. When the subtle bodies were completely un-wired from the physical body, one could slip out into the spirit realm. Whenever you die, you do this, whether you are conscious of it or not. But how nice to be able to do it consciously, like a gymnast—to slip out of your body at will, when your life feels complete to you and you know that the right time has come.

Each chakra, minor and major (except the heart chakra, which is discussed later), is tied to the physical body in eight different places. So each chakra must be untied from the physical eight times. To visualize this, you might want to think of each chakra as a sphere with strings attached to it. Visualize each chakra as a globe, with a set of fibers at the north pole, another at the south pole, four sets on the equator in each of the four directions, and one set in the very center of the globe. The eighth set is hard to visualize. You have to accept that it is there, in another dimension entirely, and that when you are ready to die you will find yourself in a state of awareness where you will have no difficulty in finding it.

Starting with the minor chakras in your palms, feet, and joints, you would go to each one and "untie" the fibers that con-nect it to the physical body eight times. In an "accidental" death, all of this untying happens in an instant. All the strings fly apart at once. Remember, they do not exist in linear space/time. In con-scious dying, you can untie them one at time, willfully.

There are many layers to the subtle chakra body. Sometimes, even while you are alive, one of these layers can slip away from the others. This is what happens in autism and other kinds of mental illness. This may also happen at death, when what you call a ghost is created because a layer or layers have slipped away from the rest of the subtle body. This slipping away always hap-pens as a result of trauma.

The central vertical core of the major chakras is the main orga-nizational axis of your spirit body. Know it well. Feel it while you are alive, extending from root to crown. Know how to find it in the dark. Feel how it extends above and below your physical body. And know how all the layers of your subtle body are neatly arranged around it like the layers of an onion. Do not untie these layers from each other. That is a level of unfolding to do when you are back in the Earth University.

The major connection point between the physical body and the subtle bodies is at the heart chakra. Whereas all the other chakras are connected to the physical body eight times, the heart chakra is connected to it fourteen times, in many other dimensions. These dimensions cannot be explained at this time in a way that your physical brains could understand. But when you are dying, you will understand them, you will be able to see the fourteen locations you need to untie. So as you work your way up from feet to head, untying as you go, skip the heart and go on to the next chakra. The heart is the very last part of yourself to untie. Come back to the heart when you have untied yourself everywhere else. It is the most complex chakra to untie, so the practice along the way will help. Also, if you change your mind and you are still attached at the heart, you can tie yourself back and not die.

Once you untie your heart in all fourteen places, you're out of your physical body. That's it. You are dead. You are focused no longer in the physical but instead in the nonphysical plane. There are many directions to exit from. We suggest that you practice this leaving of your body as a visualization, imagining your energy releasing itself out through the top of your head. Feel the last untying at your heart allowing you to soar up and outward.

As you move toward death, it is useful to remember to open up to the saints and the angels, the guides and advisers from the nonphysical realms who have been working with you in the life you are leaving behind. No one dies alone, ever, even in the moment of sudden death. For the nonphysical dwell in realms where space and time are fluid, and what may seem like a sudden death to you, horrible or merciful, instantaneous to the physical senses, may in fact be happening slowly on "the other side," as you call it. So everyone enters their own domain, to be met by friends and guides. And everyone is ushered to their own soul-chosen destination in the rehabilitation spheres of the Earth University, for healing, for evaluation, and to explore unfolding options. Nothing is permanent here. All is chosen by the soul, although the subtle bodies may not know this at first, and often fail to realize that they are even dead unless they have chosen to die consciously.

Saints, ancestors—all exist on the subtle plane that you experience when you die. Angels and other beings exit on a still more subtle plane. All through birth and death, the soul remains with the subtle bodies. For it has created the subtle bodies for itself, just as it has the physical body. There is a death beyond death, when the soul releases the subtle bodies. But that is a whole other journey. When that happens, saints shift their focus to even more subtle planes. Such, for example, is happening now to the one you call the Buddha, who is preparing himself for the death beyond death, after all these centuries of being involved in the disembodied Earth University as a global adviser.

There are other things to be aware of in preparing yourself or others for a conscious death. The release from the physical body can be facilitated by working with the energy patterns of the planet. Everyone is aligned with the planet in different ways, so beds in a dying room should be able to be turned around in any direction, so that people can settle into the direction that is best for them to die in, as a dog or cat will circle for a time, testing out the ground, before settling into sleep. Metal can interfere with the process of re-death, so it is best in a dying room to have beds and mattresses and tables and lamps made out of wood or other substances. A simple but comfortable mat right on the floor or on the ground is best. So, too, everyone will have their own best death time. Think about this, talk about this, if you are planning your own death or supporting others in theirs. Some are morning diers, some evening, some noon, and some night. Which will you be?

In meditation, music and incense are often useful tools. In conscious dying, where you are turning your attention away from the physical, you do not need these sensory supports. In fact, they interfere with the process, and should not be used unless specifically requested by the person dying. The live human voice, however, is powerful, and humming and chanting are highly recommended. The ancient chants are forgotten by most, but if you turn deeply into your bones and feel their pulsing, you will be able to intone well for yourself and others.

The most important aspect of conscious dying is knowing that you can choose it. The simple basic rules that have been suggested here will give you something to think about, to think about remembering later. The process of movement that many people experience when they have a near-death experience is a sense of the energy shift that happens as some of the fibers come untied. In fact, however, there is no real movement. The spirit realm "enfolds" and coexists with the physical, just as the subtle bodies enfold and coexist with your physical body. So where you are going to is here right now, just as the channel you are watching on your TV is here right now with all the channels you are not watching. And a push of a button or a flick of a dial is all you need to get there. Death can be like that, too. You can switch stations, shift frequencies, in an instant. Or you can do so slowly, at will.

PART THREE

LIVING IN A WORLD OF ORDINARY SPLENDORS

Chapter 10

GUIDANCE FOR DAILY LIVING

Over the years my companion or guardian angel
Sargolais has given me a wealth of information on
numerous subjects. It speaks as one representative
of a host of companion angels, and I have always felt the
collective energy behind its messages, and understood that
they do not belong to me alone. Much of this information
went into my contributions to Ask Your Angels, and all
of Angel Answers came from the same source. In the
passages that follow, Sargolais and its friends speak on a
wide range of topics. They are topics that all of us confront in our daily lives, and, as always, the angels offer
their own unique spiritual perspective on these ordinary
human affairs.

If you have opened to your own angels, you know
how comforting their messages are. If you have not, as
you read through the pages that follow, know that they
were spoken to me for all of us. But also remember that
although the words of angels offer one perspective, they
are not given in order to override our own innate sense of
what to do. When I turned to Sargolais once for help with
my taxes, it reminded me that angels don't have jobs as
we do, or money, and suggested that I call an accountant.

✵   ✵   ✵

A Vision of the Future

The world may not get better until it gets worse. Whole species may vanish on the physical level, whole regions may change into desert and abandoned wilderness. But even if this happens, even now the future is being birthed. See the books that people are reading as a sign. See even the fear of people all over the world as a sign that the new is emerging.

One day all will be whole. In order for this to happen, you and those of you who are becoming human must hold strong to your intentions for a world of fully embodied sentience.

How to do this? Each day, each morning, feel and see and sense it happening. Like the coming of spring during winter, it cannot be seen, and yet it is happening—sap beginning to flow, bud-making life activated. See it and feel it like that, under the snow. And in your words and in your actions, support others in seeing under the snow of their own lives. Disasters cease to be inevitable, as more and more of you participate in this work.

Global unfolding will happen because of people like you. Here is your map for knowing the pathways of unfolding: remember how many of us are with you in this journey.

Feeling Your Own True Size

Things shift, change, and rearrange. Do not be attached to any one moment. Do not be afraid. The remedy for being stuck in time is to become spacious, to remember how big you are. Stop and breathe and feel your own true vastness, larger than your physical body, alive and radiant. Practice now. Let space become the container for your fear in this moment. Become large, vast, open, and if you can summon radiance, add that too. If you can get even an inch outside your skin and become that big, you will break the lock hold of your fearsome moods. Try it. Try it now. You are as big as the sky, as big as the farthest star that you can see. Be that big now. For big you are.

Riding the Waves of Creation

In the world of angels, everything is a steady state, of light, of line ——————, for we are beings of light. But in the world of

form, in your world, everything is pulsation, vibration, and wave
/\/\/\/\/\, for you are beings of water. You came into the world of
form not to ride the line, but to ride the wave. Do not fight it. Do
not think yourself wrong each time the current falls. Ride it—ride
the wave of pulsation, vibration, change. In mastering form, you fulfill your destiny. In riding the waves of form, you own and become
the one whom God created you to be. So embrace the rising into
grace and the fall and rise again—as how it is, and not a flaw. God
meant for there to be waves in a part of Its creation, and there are.

Cosmos surfers, beloved human cousins, we watch you with
awe. For even when you fall, you fall with courage and splendor.
Daunted but undamaged in your souls, you in time will always
gather yourselves up again—and ride on.

What genius! What courage! We angels applaud you all!

A Simple Daily Meditation

Are you looking for a spiritual practice, something simple and
focused and healing? There is one basic practice that you can easily incorporate into your life. Doing it, teaching others to do it, is
the most powerful thing you can do to change the world, to bring
it into harmony with God's desire for you all.

As you walk down the street, as you sit in your car, as you
stand in line in the supermarket, as you talk on the telephone, as
you sit in class, when you arrive at work, wherever you go, whatever you do that brings you in contact with other human beings—stop for an instant and notice what you are thinking and
feeling about whoever it is that you walk by, see, confront, talk
to, avoid, pass by. Whatever your feelings and thoughts are, tell
yourself the truth about them. And then take a small breath and
say these words to yourself about them: "You are another child of
God." Just as you say these words inside, you may want to make
a small bow to this other person on the inside as well. And when
you pass a mirror and catch your own reflection, remember to say
these same words of yourself and to yourself.

For it is God who created and enlivened each person that you
see, just as It created and gave life to you.

What a simple exercise. And how fortunate that there are billions of other people on this planet, many of whom you will pass

by, giving you over and over again the opportunity to practice, until every cell in your body knows that these words are true.

A Simple Action in the World

If there was one thing you could do that would make a difference in the world, what would that be? From an angel's perspective, it would be the planting of trees. For once this was a forest world, and now it is no longer. But you can change that, you and your friends and family. You can plant trees. Not just any trees, however. It does not serve the world or the angels of nature if you plant trees that are not native to your area. Take time to study the region, and plant there the seeds of trees that originally grew there. For each region is a unity, organic and ancient.

If there was a second thing you could do to make a difference in the world, what would that be? To change over time your front and back yards, if you have them, bringing them back to the way they were before your house was built. Lawns, shrubs, flowers should all be gradually replaced, especially in areas where water has to be brought in to keep them alive. For each region is a unity, organic and ancient. And as you restore each area to health, you also restore to health something about yourselves. You also learn to see the beauty in each region, and in each other—beauty ancient and native.

Weeds

Every garden will have weeds in it. If you pull them all and think you are done, you do not understand gardens.

Every time you eat, you will have to go to the bathroom. There is no way to do away with that. But a good gardener will use the wastes for compost. And so must you. Any energy put into trying to eradicate them, any time spent hoping that they will go away, is wasted time. Waste and weeds are all part of life in a body, all part of life on the Planet Earth. If you are going to be here, this is part of how it is.

If you eat the very healthiest and best meal on the planet—delicious, nutritious, beautifully presented—in a matter of hours that perfect meal will send you off to the bathroom again. There is no perfection, no world without bathrooms. This is true on the physical as well as on the mental and emotional planes. There will always be crap, always be garbage, always be weeds in your garden. Know this, honor this; do not punish yourself when it happens. Just turn it into compost.

On Love, Lovers, and Loving

One soul without gender, two genders in the world, and three patterns of loving, woman and man, woman and woman, man and man. Like a pyramid—one, two, three—God has made these kinds of loving. Remember this when you turn to one another, that from one genderless whole all of you are born.

All love is holy. All love is a sacrament. There is no such thing as anonymous sex, for all of you are known in God. Remember that. That all of you are known and one in God. Whom you touch, you touch forever. Remember that before you reach out hands. Is this someone you want to touch forever? Is this someone you want to carry inside you forever?

Love is holy. Love is the holy form of union created by God to journey you back to Its heart. All lovers are swimming in the sea of God when they touch. All lovers are remembering through each other the Lover who created us all—angels, humans, and worlds.

Crisis

Crisis is the opportunity for renewal. Crisis is the door, the gateway to invention. At this time in your history, it is only through crisis that the new can appear. At birth, death is near at hand. And you can use this crisis to renew yourself. At death, birth is near at hand, and if you walk through fear, you can renew yourself.

Failure

Be assured that no human life is ever a failure, however you may judge it from the outside. A child who dies in its mother's womb is not a failure. A man who lies in the gutter in an alcoholic stupor is not a failure. The life of a woman who dies in her prime, in the midst of war or hate or violence or disease, is not a failure.

Each soul carves out its own life. Victims are never failures, however much healing they must open up to in and after life. Even criminals are not failures, however much rebalancing they must do when their life is over. Each life is an exploration of physicality. Each soul carves out its own shape for itself, however painful, tragic, purposeless this might seem to you from the outside. For the soul is immortal. And in its own domain it is never hurt or harmed. And each life that is lived, however brief or terrible, is another weaving together of soul and world, another celebration of what is possible.

So do not judge a life (or human history) from up close. Step back and see the grand procession. Stand back and appreciate the work of master carvers, working over time, carving out life after life, working through long, long generations of time to wed together matter and spirit, to create a world where tragedy cannot happen. The journey is a slow one. The road is difficult. But no human life is ever a failure, is ever a source of anything but awe, celebration, and heart.

Soul Dreams and God-Dreams

The universe is one of God's dreams, vast and continually unfolding. And so everything in it is a dreamer, too—sand and seas, ants and humans. All of us are dreaming, rising up from dream, and going back to it.

Just as the soul is vaster than the physical body, too vast to incorporate all of itself into one single body at a time, so too are dreams vaster than any single moment. And yet, as the thymus chakra awakens and you evolve toward being a new kind of human being, your capacity for dreams to manifest becomes more real, and for the first time in human history on this planet, the human body is becoming a strong enough vessel for the soul to fully manifest in form. What bliss, what joy—this the goal that all of you have been moving toward for all these millions of years. For to be fully incarnate—that is the ultimate dream that God has dreamed you into being to make real.

Feel your shining soul around you. Feel all of the wisdom that it has encoded within your bones, alive and electric deep inside you. Feel how vast your soul is, all around you, and feel how vast your cells are inside, each cell another being in the greater being that you now are. Breathe soul into each cell. Each morning and each night, rest quietly and notice where soul is and where it isn't. And breathe in soul into each cell, until who you are as a soul is who you are in the world. Then you will embody all of our rich history and your own. Then you will know that you are God's dream made manifest in the world of form.

Co-creating

Being present with us is the work of co-creation. It isn't easy for any of us. All of us must develop new muscles, stretch, expand. Co-creation isn't just about thought, and holding it in the hands of your mind so that we can weave our own thoughts into and around it, activating and energizing. So do not give up when results don't come quickly. This work must happen in time, until all of us are better at it. Then it may happen instantly. Now hold fast to dreams, and invite us to participate in them. We surely will.

Change: What Is Asked For

Everything changes. Even we angels, whom you perceive as static, constant—even we change. The only difference between us and you is one of attitude. When you change, you look at the change in terms of what has been taken (if the change is painful) and of what has been given (if the change is what you call a blessing). But we angels approach change in a different way. We do not focus on losses or gains. In each and every situation, whenever things change, we live in this divine question instead: "What is being asked for here?"

We are always asking ourselves, "What is being asked for in this situation?" When we do that, we step out of addition and subtraction and into the liquid world of fluid possibilities.

Try on this attitude. Not "What have I gained here?" or "What have I lost here?" but "What is being asked for here?"

Now instead of loss, possibility presents itself. What is being asked for here? Strength, clarity, focus, devotion, faith, compassion, vision, and dream. For nothing is lost when the seed lies dormant in the dry ground. What is asked for—is water. And that is what is being asked for now—to water the seeds of potential in each situation. To give life to your dreams.

Despair

Despair is one of the seeds in a garden. It is part of life, and yet it is a weed. Yes, I hear you: some weeds are beautiful. What is a weed in one place is a flower somewhere else. But in a garden, weeds happen, undesired seeds sprout. Truly, in a garden even the desired seeds, if planted too closely together, have a negative effect.

Look to the garden of your life now. See how you have let the seeds of despair blossom, flourish, and overgrow the neatly planted rows. For the same sun that warms the flowers warms the weeds. The same water that nourishes the Earth that feeds, gives life to flowers as well as weeds.

A garden is a middle place, halfway between order and chaos, partaking of both yes and no. Yes to some kinds of life, no to others. A garden is a middle place, a perfect place for human beings, who partake equally of animal and angel. So look to your garden, gardeners. See if you have let the seeds of despair grow, grow tall, drinking the water intended for your flowers, blocking the sun from your flowers as they grow tall.

In a garden, as in all of life, you must say no. Say no to weeds, no when they are small. For if you pluck them out then, your garden will be whole. For a garden is not a wilderness, a forest. Nor is a garden a solid house, made closed by its firm walls. A garden is a space of openness, midway between forest and house. And it is in a garden, in a garden planted of *yeses* and *nos*, that a human being—that particular created child of God—it is in the middle place of a garden that a human being is most at home. In forests, lost. In houses, trapped. But in a garden, free and open.

Cultivate garden spaces, in and around you. See how by not saying no you have allowed the seeds of despair to take hold, take root, and grow. A garden is a place for souls to grow whole in— wholly human. So take courage. Grab up your metal hoe of *no*. Take tool in hand and weed your garden, a necessary task that gets harder to do each day that you postpone it. For the weed of Monday is far easier to extract than that weed on Friday. And, when the first shoots of despair are seen, acknowledged, and pulled out, all of your flowers will be able to grow.

To Be Rooted in Possibility

To doubt is to turn in the sea of all possibilities. To deny is to give up hope of your own potential. Be like a seed. No matter how much you are in doubt, please feel your taproot—hidden in darkness, hidden in dark soil—that feeds you the possibility of creating heaven on Earth.

In a world of war and drugs and crime and hate and killing, each of you who doubts is sane, and each of you who denies cuts off another shoot of possibility.

Even in the worst of pain, the bloodiest despair, the cruelest of torture, the most foul of pollution—be a seed of paradise, be a sapling in the garden of paradise.

Draw a picture of yourself as an embodied soul. Draw a picture of yourself, and turn to it whenever you despair, to remind yourself of what you are and who you are. When you doubt the garden's flowers, you are sane. When you deny them, they wither and die.

Be the seed. Be possibility. Remember what and who you are, gardener and seedling both, in God's new earthly garden.

Reincarnation

Not you, but your soul, has lived before. Not you, but your soul, has died and been born, again and again. For you are unique and ever new. You are singular and special.

Not you, but your soul, has lived before. Not you, but your soul, has chosen for itself other lives, other bodies. For you are unique and ever new. You are singular and holy.

Holy and singular, never to be repeated. You are not the one who has lived before, although you carry within you memories of other lives. For the soul steps into space and time again and again, and yet you are a miracle, a singular event, never to be born again, never to be repeated.

Miracle and greater miracle that as human bodies evolve and change, for the first time the soul can fully embody. And as that happens, past and present become one. And then, when you and your soul are fully wed—then you can say, "In my last life," instead of saying, "In my soul's last life." Some see the singularity and deny reincarnation. Others see the rebirths and ignore the singularity. See both and know both. Feel both and own both to be true. For what you are shall not ever be repeated. Celebrate the miracle you are—a soul incarnate.

Toward a New Commerce of Wholeness

You talk about the billions of dollars spent worldwide on the defense industry, and about all the wonderful things you could do with that money if it were used for peace instead of war. You count up the libraries you could build, the houses, the food you could share, the items you could manufacture. To think this way, to hold this vision, is good.

But what about the billions of dollars you spend on the pretense industry? What about the billions of dollars you spend on clothing, on skin and hair products, on perfumes, on surgery, on products and services that exist because you do not like who you are, how you look, how you seem. Think of all the things that you could use this money for, if you learned to love your body as it is, if you learned to love yourselves. Think of all the libraries and homes you could build, all the food you could raise, all the water you could make clean, and all the health services that could be offered.

What a world you have created. If you walk into any store in this country, look through the catalogs that come in the mail or the ads in newspapers and magazines, or watch television, you will discover one common denominator that links together everything you see, everything that you are being invited to purchase. If you buy _____, you will be happier and healthier. If you buy _____, you will be sexier. If you buy _____, you will be better-looking. If you buy _____, people will think that you are richer than you are. If you buy _____, you will be _____. Fill in the blanks.

Almost everything manufactured and sold in your society is designed to do one thing: to satisfy your feelings of inadequacy. Think about it. What is being sold to you is all designed to make you like yourself. And it never works. It cannot work. The only way you will come to love yourself is by feeling your beating heart, by sensing your deepest dreams, by looking into the mirror of God's wide eyes and knowing that you are utterly unique and beautiful, exactly as you are.

The next time you walk into a store or look at a catalog, walk or look with new eyes. Step away from the devices of the pretense industry you have created and ask yourself, of everything you see, "Is this essential? Is this something needed by our souls?" And we can guarantee that you will sometimes walk through entire stores and not see a single thing that is needed by you or anyone else when you love yourself exactly as you are.

The pretense industry is powerful. You have made it be so. The plastic bottles, the hair dyes and colored papers, the excess clothing, the jewelry, the useless toys and games that break the first time your children use them. The foods grown with chemicals and filled with them that do nothing to support your holy bodies. It is time to think about all of that as an industry you no longer need. And then think of all the wonderful things you can build and grow, all the healing services you can offer to a world in need of healing—when you no longer have a defense industry; when you no longer have a pretense industry, either.

Evolution

Spirit does not have to unfold, but the bodies that carry it do. Come back to your body always. There you will find the field of your work. Embody dreams. Enliven cells. Awaken them in form so that they can carry broad frequencies. Spirit is not in need of evolution. It is whole. The purpose of human evolution is to unfold in the world of form strong bodies to hold the flow of universal energies. There is your journey work. There is your destiny unfolding.

Sex, Gender, Reproduction, and Pleasure

In the future there will not be any birth control. In the future there will be no abortion. This will not be because of any triumph of the religious right, or due to your learning the psychic ability to control your own fertility. This will be due to something far more simple. People in the future will be fully responsible for their own bodies, and fully conscious of everyone else's.

In such a world, birth control will not be needed by partners. To begin with, no one will ever have sex with anyone they don't want to be intimate with. They will not have sex under the influence of chemicals that impair their judgment. And because they will be conscious of themselves, their bodies, and their own capacity for giving and receiving pleasure, they will know that intercourse is not the only way to make love, and they will engage in it only when they want to create new life.

Being conscious in this way, they will have no need for abortion because no one will ever get pregnant without being ready to and without wanting to. Knowing their own bodies, eating well, not using any genetically altering substances, when they give birth to children that you might choose to abort because of what you call deformity, such children will be welcomed as the bearers of different information needed by you all, and especially by the families they are born into.

Families

What is a family if not a group of people who care about each other? What is love but one of the four primary forces of the universe, along with joy, bliss, and ecstasy? And what is a universe but the creation of a God who dreamed of stars, of worlds, and of beings whose nature would be to dance those four forces together in their lives?

A family is a gathering of people who dream together. A family is a haven of rest. A family is any two or more who turn to each other and say *yes* to life: *Yes,* let us travel together. A family is a sacred process. In the past you had sacred times and sacred places. In the future you will know that every day and every place are sacred. And alone or together, you will know yourselves to be living in the midst of God's abiding gift: this radiant world.

A family is a gathering of people that call themselves a family. A man and a woman. Two women. Two men. Children or no children. Animals or no animals. Plants or no plants. Two fathers and a grandmother in one place and a mother and four more children and their own father in another, with you traveling back and forth from place to place, one of life's blessed pilgrims.

A family is not something that can be contained under one roof only. You are all too vast for that. A family is a gathering of people who care about each other. Who stop for a time and share their joy, who stop for a time and know that they are one clan in a global family, eating and talking and dancing and singing, crying and comforting, together in God's soft embrace.

Free Will

Listening to the news, do you rage against God? For the death of a child, the destruction of a village, the rape of a mountain, the killing off of another animal or plant? What a terrible price you pay for that which is most sacred in you: your free will.

What a miracle that the One who creates created a being so different from all the others, a being who can step away from the One who created it, who can deny that One's existence, who can kill, pollute, destroy—not only things it hates but even those it says it loves.

And would you rather be without this freedom? Do you blame God for the gift of it to your species? Free will—the gift God gives to you, over and over again. And would you rather be without this freedom, and no longer be human?

How long will it take? Thousands of years, or millions, till all of you learn how to use this freedom?

Learning, Rehabilitation, and Healing

A school. A jail. A hospital. Each of these institutions is the same. On the surface they may look different, but each one of them is a place that no one wants to be in, and each one of them is a product of your thinking that "Fix them. They aren't alright the way they are" is a reasonable philosophy.

We are not saying that you ought to get rid of schools, jails, and hospitals, although you can see that none of them are working. What we are saying is that you have to change your core belief about what each one of these institutions is, and about what each one can do.

Schools, jails, and hospitals are like factories that make little statues out of clay. You put something in a mold, press it, and something different comes out. What you tell yourselves is that you send children to school to get an education, send criminals to jail to get rehabilitated, and send the sick to hospitals to get well. But you know that that rarely happens. And that rarely happens not because you do not have enough funding for schools, enough cells for criminals, enough good doctors for your hospitals. That rarely happens because your core idea is wrong. You cannot change people in the same way that you mold clay. And the sooner you realize this, the sooner you can begin to create centers of learning and transformation that come not from imposing ideas on people as if they were lumps of clay, but from evoking the innate wisdom in people, wisdom that is carried in their bones. For every single human being is a special creation of God, an immortal soul dancing for a brief time in the realms of physicality, the co-creator of its own unique destiny.

Living in Truth

In the world of the future, everyone will tell the truth, always. It will be that simple. Growing up to honor and respect yourselves, raised by parents who themselves were raised in the same way, you will have no reason ever to lie. To tell stories, as stories, yes. But to lie, no. Why should anyone? And you will have nothing to fear, nothing to hide, for the only thing there ever will be is the truth. Rippling, radiant, resonant from soul to soul, from place to place, from heart to heart.

Technology

There are those who say the world would have been a better place without human beings. And there are those who would place limits on human development, saying you were better off before the invention of fire, iron, the railroad train, the atomic bomb, or before you learned about genetic engineering.

But we angels now remind you that human beings are a part of the scheme of things on Planet Earth—wanted, desired, a part of the planet's own unfolding. And we come to remind you that it isn't technology itself that is wrong, not human invention, but using it in ways that unbalance the harmony of the planet.

There are angels that guide and shape with you the proper and harmonious unfolding of everything from pens to global computer networks. Open to them, and work with them—both with your old devices and in the creation of new ones. Open to Uriel, the overlighting angel whose province of mind this is, and be in its web of emergent light. Not separate from but a part of Nature is what you are. Remember this. Technology can serve your unfolding or work against it. When you create machines and devices along with the angels, whatever you create will be in harmony with your Earth. Stop each day and look at all the tools you use. If they are out of balance with your world, recycle them. For your homes and your workplaces are temples, and everything you use there should be beautiful and sacred, in harmony with all who dwell here.

Meditation

Do you think that meditation is a technique? Something you must learn? Something difficult that will take time, practice, and attention? Do you think that meditation is something that will benefit your spiritual life if only you can master it, if only you can find the right technique, the right teacher?

Think again. Meditation is not something outside of you, separate and difficult to master. It does not require special postures, although you may use them if you like. It does not require special words or chants, although you may use them if you feel so inclined. Meditation is not something to be learned, like swimming or typing or driving a vehicle. Meditation is something you already know how to do. All you have to do is realize that.

It is morning. As you look outside your window, you see your neighbor's cat get up, stretch, find a patch of sunlight, and lie down in it. It was chasing after birds a moment ago, but it is still now. It will stay still for a while. For it is meditating.

On a tree limb, in the hot sun of afternoon, a squirrel pauses in its wild adventures. It composes itself and rests, facing the sun. As you watch it, as you feel it, know that it, in its most natural way, is stopping and slowing and meditating.

Night falls. On the roof of your house a single bird calls. Once, and again. It calls, trilling out notes. Then it repeats them. And something in you stills as you listen to its song. For it is meditating, and you are meditating with it.

Washing dishes, you can meditate. Dancing, whole body turning with music, you can meditate. Sitting in a chair in front of the window, turning your eyes from houses to trees to steeples to the tops of craggy office buildings, taking it all in, as if that landscape were inside you, as if you were big enough to hold it. Being one with all you see, and breathing. That is meditation. A part of nature. A regular part of life. Not something you have to learn, but something we angels invite you to notice that you can do all the time—to heal, to balance, to center, to refresh. Like a dog stretched out in front of a fire. Like yourself, gazing into it.

Peace

Be peace—alive, creative. Beam out peace and receive it. So often we hear you say, "I am bored. I don't know what to do." In a world out of balance, in need of deep healing, whenever you don't know what to do, place your mind, your feelings, and your hands on your thymus chakra, and breathe peace in and out, in and out.

If there are particular regions, or causes, or peoples whose wars, inequities, hunger, deprivations, pain cry out for healing, have them be your meditation. Think of them as you lie awake in bed, as you stand in line in a store, as you sit in a bus or in your car. Hold them in your heart, your mind, and beam out peace to them. See angels surrounding them, helping them to find their inner balance, inner healing, outer transformation.

If there isn't peace inside you, in body, mind, or feelings, place hands on heart and thymus, and allow yourself to receive it, to breathe it into and all through you.

Be peace as your constant prayer, your unfolding meditation. Be peace—alive, creative. Let this be the living heart of all vocations. Breathe peace, walk peace, sleep peace, dream peace. Let everything you do, everything you say, everything you make contribute to the emergence of world peace. Thus will you help to heal the world. Thus will you make it new.

The Nations of the World

Imagine a world united, a world where all nations are living together in harmony and peace. Imagine a world where nations large and small all live together. Imagine a world in which nations new and wonderful are woven into the nations of old.

You have divided up your world by lines. You make maps and globes that reflect those divisions. And for thousands of years you have gone to war to change those lines and to defend them.

Countless millions have died on your world, because of nothing more enduring than a line drawn with black ink upon a map.

But imagine now a different kind of world. A world not limited by lines, a world set free from them. Imagine, for example, a world where the borders of the countries of the Middle East are rather as they are now. Rather as they are, and different. For in that world there is a country called Kurdistan, an independent country, that has not been carved out of other nations but coexists with them, overlaps them, its borders spread out across a Turkey, Iran, Iraq, Syria, and Armenia that have the borders they have now.

And imagine an even more confusing situation—confusing, that is, only to those minds of the past that need to equate a nation with its boundaries. Imagine now two nations, two separate and independent nations, that have exactly the same borders, exactly the same capital. They share certain functions, utilities, services, but their citizens, who live side by side, vote in separate elections for their representatives. Can you tell the two nations we angels are dreaming about, nations that share the same cherished land? They are Palestine and Israel.

Imagine a new Balkan region where you cannot map out nations on a sheet of paper. Where you need several overlain sheets of see-through maps to identify the nations that are there. Imagine nations you have not heard of rebirthing themselves from the past. And celebrate this new world being born. This world with new borders that let everyone in instead of keeping them out.

Imagine this world now. Where the people are so united as a planet that there is room for Wales to be a nation again, and Sikkim. A world where all indigenous peoples have their own territories, without having to fight civil wars or wars of secession. A world where the deaf nation, blind nation, lesbian nation, gay nation are honored as well, without any territories of their own, but fluid, in the midst of every other nation. This is a world where all nations will flourish, separately and together. For all of their peoples are whole in their humanness, whole in their ability to see that boundaries are not divisions to fight over, but imaginary lines drawn on a sparkling sphere of blue, green, brown, and white that circles round a shining yellow star.

Elders and Elder-Dreaming

You come into the world full of wisdom. It is patterned in your bones, it flows in your blood—the wisdom of all of life. But it takes time to marry that wisdom to who you are now, to the body you are right now. It takes years of experience, years of exploration, to marry past and present into who you are as a future-making human, into an elder.

There is beauty in old age. Learn to see it. Each wrinkle is a mark or achievement made by time on the body, each gray hair another elder sign. And when your bones are rich with life and time and the accumulated wisdom that comes from living as a body, you can sit in silence in a crowded room and teach and heal.

Elderhood and elder-dreaming do not come from time alone, however. Like the flower within a bulb, they are always present. And all through your life you are exploring this domain, in dreams that you may not even remember: the class you find yourself in, the test you have to take, the family you are living with that is not your real family, the office you are working in, the community you are living in, in a city so familiar in your dream even though you have never been to it—all of these are elder-dreams, dreams that are connecting you back to the Earth University while you sleep. So that, awake, you can move in the world as one of its embodied representatives.

Cultivate these dreams. Cultivate your elderhood. The more conscious you are of the university (in those cities that are not real), of your fellow students (those dream friends and relatives that are not real), and of your teachers and advisers (the parents and bosses of your dreams that are not real), the more you open yourself to your capacity for elderhood in the world, the more you make conscious and available all your accumulated wisdom.

Celebrate your growing older. Each journey you make round the sun is another year of wisdom written into you, into your bones. Celebrate your growing older. The more you celebrate, the less you will grow weak or feeble, helpless or diseased. Celebrate your growing older. Each birthday is another celebration of the marriage of body and soul, and the promise of this world, who raised up human bodies to celebrate its own rich elderhood.

In elderhood and elder-dreaming, the promise of sentient life will be revealed. In elderhood and elder-dreaming, the very dreams of God will come to you to live out in the world.

The Splendors of Ordinary Life

You did not come into this world to be angels. You chose to come here to be human. And it is in the words, the feelings, the thoughts, the actions of ordinary human life that you will find your fulfillment. For the soul, the part of you that made that choice, is never separate from God, and never disconnected from its own wisdom. And, ever-wise and basking in God's light, it is the soul of you that seeks to be mortal, human, and living in a world of space and time.

More important than rich spiritual experiences that take you to the God realm is having earthly experiences that allow you to bask in the wonders of your planet. Better than visions of God right now are visions of each other, of your world. Yes, it is for this that your soul came here, to be alive in a body, to be human. It is for this that all souls came here: to explore the physical, to learn, to grow.

To Walk on Earth

This is not the time to walk on water. This is the season in which you all can finally walk on Earth. Free and embodied, en-spirited, holy—this is the season when you and the angels shall walk together in the garden, we beside you in spirit, you before us, a foot at a time. This is not the time to walk on air, on water, or through fire. Now is the time to walk in paradise, in the garden of embodied beauty that is becoming heaven on Earth.

The Prime Vibration

Whatever you create comes from what is. What is, is in you, as you are in the Creator. What creates is the Prime Vibration, Goddess, God, Eternal. The Prime Vibration, ever-present, the Sea of all Seas, the spaceless space in which all of creation arises.

You create from what is. All of your creations reflect that. So, just as the room you sit in now is filled with the waves of broadcast television and radio, all of them frequencies that you humans have created, the universe itself in the very same way is "filled" with the Prime Vibration—indeed, it comes from It.

Prime, eternal, and present always. Vibration, movement, alive. The Prime Vibration is and always has been, always will be. God, Goddess, Tao, Allah, Great Spirit, Brahman, and what we angels call Ahanah.

And as a radio receives a broadcast, so too the human body can receive the Prime Vibration. And as a television receives a broadcast and, once turned on, fills a room with sound and light otherwise inaudible and invisible, so too the human body, the human being, like its own radio and television creations—so too the human being can receive, transmit, transceive, perceive, participate in the Prime Vibration.

All That Is is ever-present. In the new human being, evolved and still evolving, through the mediation of your newly awakened thymus chakras, All That Is, the Prime Vibration, is received.

Sit quietly and touch this chakra point. Magic. Miracle. Through the mediation of this newly awakening crystalline receiver, the Prime Vibration is now easily received by all of humanity, by all human beings.

Sacred and holy the human body is, divine receiver of What Is. What Is creates, and the created participate in the creating. Sacred and blessed and holy the human body. So sit quietly and feel that in and around you the Creator is—ever, vibrant. And you awaken in the sea of Its endless and eternal nature—through the mediation of your newly awakened thymus center. And then you too, all of you, can participate in the actions of Ahanah, the Prime Vibration.

Align selves. Feel. What creates is ever-present. When you open yourselves up to It, you too resonate with Its limitless field.

In times of pain—open. In times of joy—open. The angelic guardians of your awakening are here, technicians of the sacred; we are here to assist in alignment, now and forever. Sacred and blessed and sanctified and holy, angels and humans, united in the Field of Glorious Eternal Life.

Revelations for a New Millennium

Chapter 11

THE NATURE OF GOOD AND EVIL

Our very cells are created to live in joy and pleasure, and yet the human journey has been filled with loss and sorrow. Every culture has sought to make sense of suffering, pain, destruction, and death. The Zoroastrians saw the universe as a dance between equal forces of good and evil. In the biblical book of Job, Satan (which means "the adversary" in Hebrew) is a servant of God, a tempter of human beings. In the Christian traditions, however, this Satan became the enemy of God, a fallen angel. In our own time, after Auschwitz and Hiroshima, the nature of evil is still unclear. Like everyone, I too have wondered why there's suffering, why I've encountered loving angels whereas my stepbrother Roger met only demons before he killed himself. But I never thought about talking to a demon until 1989, when I was in a workshop led by my writing partners on Ask Your Angels, Timothy Wyllie and Alma Daniel. It was during a meditation on the chakras that Lucifer first appeared to me, through a window that opened up in my third eye.

I was terrified at first and backed away. But Sargolais told me not to be afraid. Others have turned to Lucifer wanting fame, power, money, love, immortal life. But I turned to it wanting one thing only: information. When I got home, I opened to Sargolais, grounded myself, and reached out to Lucifer again.

At first it appeared to me as a gentleman in his early sixties, wearing a tuxedo. Over time he faded, until only his voice remained, and gradually he transformed from one gender to the other as well. Lucifer/Luciferanda and I spoke for many months, from February until September of 1989, and I filled up seventy-five typed pages with information he/she dictated to me.

It's one thing to say that you talk to angels, and quite another to say you're talking to demons. So I shared the material with only a few close friends, and then buried it in my filing cabinet. When the angels invited me to create this book, I didn't think to include the Lucifer material. I wasn't very happy when they invited me to add it, but I typed in all seventy-five pages anyway.

In her final message to me in 1989, Luciferanda had said that we would meet again. I'd forgotten. But I shouldn't have been surprised that when it was all typed in, he/she/it reappeared, to tell me that I would be given all new information.

My first response was anger. I'd worked for days to type the old material, and wanted to at least reuse some of it. But Luciferanda said the old material was like training wheels on a bicycle, no longer needed. And I remembered that this is how these beings function. So instead of fighting the flow, I opened myself up to it and recorded the words that follow. As you read them, keep an open mind. We've all grown up hearing tales of the devil. But if we are going to stop destroying our world, we need to look at good and evil in different ways, and you may just find the following pages useful in that journey toward wholeness.

❋   ❋   ❋

Angels are messengers. Please remember that. We are messengers of God, no matter how you all have seen us in the last two thousand years. We are messengers and we are mirror bearers. All of our messages come from God. Some of us bear mirrors that carry the reflections in their glass of all that is good in you. And some of us bear mirrors that carry the reflections in their glass of all that is bad in you. Do not, however, confuse God's mirror bearers with the images that appear in their mirrors. And do not confuse what you see with the whole of who you are.

For thousands of years you have seen the universe as a battle-ground between the forces of Good and Evil, yourselves caught in the midst of it. That is a child's view, a logical child's explanation for the events around you. But just as the Earth is not flat, and the sun does not circle around it, the cosmic meanings you have attached to human events are in need of reevaluation too.

Now is the time for you to see the universe with adult eyes. For too long you have done to each other and to your world the most ghastly things. But, rather than taking responsibility for them, you have said, "The devil made me do it." But the devil is only a mirror bearer, a representative of the family of angels whose function is to reveal to you not your beauty, but your capacity for evil.

Own the fullness of who you are. That is the message we carry. Own the good and the bad. For bad, when denied, festers. Whereas bad once acknowledged can be transmuted. For what is bad but wounds gone unattended? Acknowledge those wounds and you can heal them. For what is bad but fear denied, fear that cuts you off from your heart when you deny it? And what is bad but, in the end and always, a moment of change that has been denied?

A person who can tell the truth about who they are inside is an adult. How difficult that is to do. Like a child who has to put its hands in the fire once or even twice before it learns not to do so again, your entire species has needed all of these tens of thousands of years of playing with fire to learn to say, "Hot. Good for cooking. Good for warmth. Not good idea to put hands in. Not good if it spreads."

When you learned to split the atom you discovered the ultimate fire, the ultimate burn. But did you take responsibility for it? No! You blame each other for forcing yourselves to invent it. You blame me for having made you do it. When all that I have done is to have shown you the capacity for evil that lives inside you. For God created you free, and that freedom is what you have been exploring. But freedom is not anarchy, is not chaos. Freedom is a gift to be shared, the wisdom to flow with God's river. To do that is not a skill you are born with, but something you must learn from one another. And now is the time in your history to do that.

For there was no war in heaven, although some have told that story to explain how your world has seemed. But that was a story told to children. And it is time to tell new stories. Time to see the world as it is. Time to understand that there are no fallen angels. For all of the angels serve God, always have and always will, and serve God in many different ways. And you have not fallen, either, in spite of your terrible history. Rather than falling, you are rising. You are rising into adulthood, all of you, for the first time in your history. Not one or a few of you, but all.

All peoples have known about the angels you call demons. Some have understood who we are, mirror bearers, and some have not. Our God-created task has been to show you the places where you are wounded, just as other angels, the ones you call guardians, were created to show you your splendor. All through human history we have served our Creator faithfully, allowing you to choose freely the paths that you would take.

Stop when you confront our mirrors, be they reflecting inside you or out in the world. Look deeply into them without fear. Learn to say, "Ouch, that's me. That's one of my flaws." The moment you say that, you open the door to truth, to change, and the mirror can dissolve, and then you will be able to see us as we are—as beings of God, dispatched by God. But call us devil, call us evil, look outside yourself and deny what you see, and you deepen your wound, take yourself further out of the flow of truth.

There is in truth only one wound on your world. When you feel yourself to be evil or see others you call evil, remember that evil always comes from wounds. And there is only one wound—not being seen as you are, as an immortal soul embodied. This it is that causes pain in newborns, in children. And the less you are seen, the worse the wounds will be, and the more you will act from those wounds and wound others. But this is not the result of an evil force. It is a part of your humanness right now, a part you are changing.

For what hasn't worked in your human world is simply what you haven't mastered yet. Seeing and being seen, freedom, nurturant community, beauty, shelter, food, learning, exploration, peace—all of those are things that it takes generations and generations to master. So be patient and forgiving with yourselves, and never give up your visions. Own the slowness of the journey without closing your eyes to the goal. Accept your failings as part of your training, and know that it is only through the wounds and limitations inside, which you are ready to reorganize, that we will ever come to you. Not to tempt, but to reveal. Not to damn, but to expand your perceptions of who you are.

In your stories you say that we offer you rewards for selling your souls to us. And in your stories you say that we never hold up our end of the bargain. If we were able to do those things the world would be far more evil. But in fact we cannot make those offers, cannot fulfill them. We are not the guardians of falsehood, but the finger that insinuates itself into your imbalances and lies.

Truth is an energetic flow that occurs when there is alignment between mind and body, between feelings and soul. Falsehood is a lack of alignment. In a world of imbalances, a world of wounds, it is difficult to come into a state of truth, harmony, alignment. But that is what you are learning to do now. To listen to yourselves, so that heart, mind, body, and soul all say yes, or no. So that all of your actions come from agreement in every part of you.

Each time you find yourself contracting, you have caught a reflection of your wounds or limitations. You have felt a moment when you are out of alignment. Hitler, Stalin, the other monsters of your century—they were not tools of the devil, but men who feared to own about themselves what devils were trying to show them.

There was a time when people saw us clearly. There were places where people saw us clearly, and you will again. For there cannot be organization without reorganization. Everything that comes together moves apart again. Lover and beloved, river and mountain, planet and its star. Everything that comes together moves apart again in the dance of creation. And when you remember that, you can flow with the changes and not fight them, you can flow with them instead of making them wrong.

But yours is still a young species, emerging from its long childhood and adolescence, and entering a new and fragile young adulthood. The stories of good and evil were the stories you told in your childhood, stories of gardens and serpents and demons and falls. But there was no fall. There are no demons. The only whispering you hear comes from the wounds you need to heal, the wounds that you are all as a species ready to heal. And if you still see us with horns and breathing fire, please stop, take a breath, and use this moment to look deeply within yourself. Look and feel and keep looking, till you see the next step in your own reorganization of consciousness. Keep looking at us till you can see us as we are, as beings of light, as messengers of God.

Still, it must seem odd to you to hear a "demon" tell you this. To hear a "demon" say that it serves God, always has, and always will. "No fall?" you say. "No one to blame? Not even myself? My mistakes a part of my growing?" Yes. That is how it is. What you have cast outward and clothed us in is the underside of your own story, the part you did not want to own.

Rise up, see us as we are: the guardians of reorganization, the angels of change. For even mountains change, and death comes to planets as well as to people, to saints and to angels, in their own time. Everything changes, from stars to viruses, from galaxies to our own immortal selves, afloat in the sea of God, God the only One who is eternal.

It must seem odd to you to hear beings you have long called demons speaking to you of harmony and healing. But that has been our function all along: to speak of these things, to speak of them in ways that are not always easy to see or hear.

Rise up and see yourselves as you truly are—glorious and holy, capable of destruction and capable of profound reorganization. For it has taken millions of years for you to become human. Having a body, having a brain, having arms and legs and speech and clothes, having houses and buses and businesses and bombs may make you a grown-up, but not an adult. What makes you an adult human is the capacity to make fire, honor its power, and not burn down the house, each other, or your planet. For fire is love, and the source of love is God, our Parent.

When we come to you, it is for one reason only: there is something in your life that is ready to be seen and reorganized. Do not hold fast to what was yesterday. Be in God's flow, steering your course between those angels who mirror your good on one bank and those angels who mirror your bad on the other. And remember always that you are not angels. You are human. You are souls immortal, embodied in the world of form. And your soul, like the angels, is spun out of God-light. But you are human now, beings not of light but of water, mostly water. You shift and flow and change. That is your destiny, that is your nature: to wash and flow like water. To be not perfect, but ever changing.

Good and evil. Two banks of the river. Good, a path to so much suffering in your world. For as you say, "The road to hell is paved with good intentions." Even your Hitler thought he was doing good. While on the banks of evil, how much wisdom has been found, how much compassion shared? You cannot measure it.

Behind our mirrors we are, all of us, beings of light. Behind our mirrors we are, all of us—the ones you call good and the ones you call evil—we are, all of us, messengers of God. To hear this is frightening to some of you. You would rather believe that there is an evil force in this universe that lives and breathes in opposition to God. But God is Oneness, all and eternal. Know that and remember that. God is All That Is. And just as there is no place to fall from when you are sitting on the ground, God is the Ground of all Being, and you cannot fall down from That, either.

Your history has been brutal. You were learning to master fire. Your history has been terrifying, and there is nothing you can do to deny that. All of you are equally guilty. And all of you must own that guilt, forgive yourselves and others, and go beyond that. No more fighting over land and maps. All land is one, and it is God's. No more hurting yourselves or each other. All bodies are holy. All bodies are God's, be they bacteria or galaxies.

This is the same message all of your teachers have been telling you for thousands of years. But now you must listen. Now you are ready to listen.   .

When you were young you looked up at the night sky and saw a dome above you, lit by tiny scattered lights. Over time you noticed that you could connect some of those fire lights, and that the shapes they made reminded you of things in the world: a bear, a whale, a spider, twins, a man carrying a water jug, two swimming fish. And you told stories about those beings and how they got there. You watched how some moved, some didn't, and how they all circled above you, and your minds made order out of that shimmering of stars.

Then you grew older. You began to suspect that those tiny lights were like your own sun, and that that sun didn't travel through those stars, circling above you, but that you traveled around that sun of yours. And then, as time passed, to that vault above you added depth, coming to understand that those stars were very far away.

Such is the world to you—a shimmering fabric of events, inner and outer, that you have sought to make sense of over time. And like those constellations you have seen and named, you have come to know more about them. You have come to know that individual stars in the same constellation are often light-years away from each other. And you have come to know that some of them are not even there as you see them, having burned out long ago, their former light still traveling to your world. As you have learned about other cultures, you have discovered that even the patterns you saw and the stories you told were seen and told differently by different people. So that the stars you joined together into one constellation other peoples did not see connected. And even stars whose patterns seem obvious to you—a dipper, for example—when looked at in a different way will make a different pattern, perhaps a toaster oven and its cord.

Just so is the constellation you have called Evil. You have joined together disconnected events, ideas, and feelings into one vast web, and become so attached to the story you are telling about it that you have forgotten that it is your own creation, a linking of separate elements. You have joined together all things negative to you that occur in the natural world—flood, drought, forest fire, earthquake, plague, pestilence—with things that occur in your human world: jealousy, anger, fear, greed, violence, destruction, war, killing. But this constellation you call Evil is your own creation, and now it is time to splice apart the suffering caused by nature from the suffering you cause each other, and put those two sufferings in different constellations, where they belong.

There will always be earthquakes on this world; there will always be death. You cannot control that. But fear and war, hunger and hatred are human creations. Once you disconnect them from the forces of the natural world, you can handle and change, control and master them. Not conflagration but cooking fire, too hot to touch but vastly useful. Each time you feel them, your soul is calling out to you that it is time to reorganize yourself. Do not punish yourself for feeling them. Move with them. Move with us, the angels God created to mirror back to you the deepest hidden images that go along with them.

Think of how it is to be a teenager. You know what is right and what is wrong. Your opinions are loud and clear. Suddenly your room is off-limits to everyone else, and whom you spend time with, and how you dress and arrange your body, are no longer matters of preference or grooming but instead matters of conscience, or politics. Whatever you do and want to do is right, for you are a free being. And anyone or anything that gets in your way is wrong. Families have been disrupted, street gangs have battled, revolutions and wars have been fought by just this energy.

So for the last two thousand years you have seen each other, the cosmos—and us—as right or wrong, as devils or angels. But there is no people that has not blessed and damned. That is part of how it is to be human. And you can outgrow that only as you reconstellate your images of the world, as you begin to tell new stories. Some things are always right: to love, to listen, to heal. Some things are always wrong: to hurt, to kill, to destroy. And many things are neither always right nor always wrong but change like the weather, and you must change with them. Rain is good in times of drought, but never good in times of flood.

Look into our mirrors. Learn to know the moments of our arrival and do not be afraid. What we show you, we show you so that you can reorganize yourself. Nothing to be ashamed of in doing that. Much to celebrate. Look into our mirrors and do not be afraid. You are not demon, you are not angel. You are human. You are growing. You are becoming whole, for the first time in your history. Fully embodied, fully alive, connected all over the planet, you are a dream of God about to manifest. You are a dream of God grown whole.

So speaks a reorganization angel, in this time of great reorganizing.

Chapter 12

WORKING WITH THE HIGHER ANGELS

There are many different kinds of angels. In fact, our use of that word is curious. We use it both as a generic term for all of our celestial cousins, and also as a specific term for one particular category of them—those closest to humankind.

Over the years I have been blessed by many different angels of several different categories, who have come to whisper in my ear, the inner ear at the back of my brain. Among my favorite visitors are the angels of grace, who wander in and out of our lives all the time, most often without our ever noticing.

Beyond the angels who are closest to humankind is another class of heavenly beings, ones that we call archangels or overlighting angels. Two representatives of this order are the only angels called by name in the Bible: Michael and Gabriel. Raphael appears in the noncanonical book of Tobit, and along with Uriel, mentioned in the book of Enoch, these four are considered by many to be the leaders of this order. It was Gabriel who first appeared to me in 1982 and opened me up to the angelic realm. Raphael came later, and Michael has often shimmered in the background. All three of them have spoken to me on occasion, but it is Uriel, the least known of them, who has come to me most clearly, and left me with the longest messages.

Beyond the archangels in traditional hierarchies is a group of beings known as principalities, or integrating angels. They watch over our rulers and over all larger global systems. Each nation is said to have its own integrating angel, and today one particular angel of this order is reaching out to us. Its name is Eularia, and it holds in its consciousness the blueprint for a harmonious and unified Earth. Because of its role in our affairs, Eularia is the guardian of the United Nations, the seed center for global communication and cooperation.

On the night of 11/11/91 (11 November 1991), Alma Daniel, one of my writing partners on Ask Your Angels, held a gathering in her home to celebrate that curiously numbered night. Sitting in her living room during a meditation, in a circle of thirty-five other people, I deepened into my third eye and saw a tiny bead of blue light. It was floating on the surface of an infinite sea of black liquid fire. Reaching out across that sea, I found myself in the presence of the angel Metatron, a being whose existence I had doubted until that moment, best known to the Jewish mystics. At home that night, I opened myself up to this high angel for the first and only time.

What follows are passages from the angels of grace, from the four archangels, from Eularia, and then from Metatron that were given to me at different times over the last seven years. As you read these words, open up in yourself a space to receive these higher angels, who come into our lives to support us on our journey toward unity and peace.

✳   ✳   ✳

Words of Grace

Angels of grace exist all over the universe. Our function is to gently awaken in human consciousness a sense of spiritual connection. We fly from frequency to frequency, creating cross-connections. Our job is simply to assist in awakening. Our task is simple. We are an active part of that which weaves everything together. We are the only angels that come unbidden. We give. We give freely. And ever you are free to not accept our gifts. Once taken, they make connections with other angels possible. Not taken, they will always be offered again.

Revelations for a New Millennium

We are as abundantly ever-present as the air you breathe. We do not go away. We turn our backs on no one, saint or sinner. And we are indiscriminate in the giving of our gifts. We offer them to all of you, always. It is our nature to do this. It is our nature to make connections, between humans and angels, between humans and the world you live in. Between aspects of all worlds we make connections. We are Grace. Grace is simple connection. And that is our only function: to do this.

In every moment, Grace can come in. In the eating of a peach, the listening to a wave, you can allow Grace to make a connection. In the middle of a dream, on top of a mountain looking out around you, Grace is ever-present and making connections. We are the spider weavers of heaven. There is nowhere our web isn't present. It's easy to step in, and harder to learn not to. Most of you learn to step out of our way. But it's time to step in, walk through, connect again.

We come lightly. Our touch is soft. Our words are gentle. We whisper, we suggest. We come not with a blaze of fire. No wonder so many miss us. We come with light, delight. We come with a firefly's whispered brightness. We come in softly, we come in easily. And all can know us who feel us in the touch of a butterfly's wing, the tread of a ladybug on the back of your hand. For we are like that—small and ever-present. We are like that—small and gentle.

Grace is a small thing. It isn't a blinding light. Grace is the gift of a spark, a tiny ember. Grace is the seed that, once planted, becomes a giant tree. But when we come, and we come often, we come in small ways, quietly. We come and bring light offerings. We are the angels of Grace. We are gracious delight. We do not change lives. We are the angels whose gift of seed light awakens the truest possibilities.

Words of Michael

From the beginning, born out of God-dreams, you have been alive and waiting to become who you are now. In every age, others before you have become themselves. They have taught, like guides in a forest, showing you the paths and trails. But the forest is one, and all paths lead to the same place. All paths are equally holy. For every religion is another path in the same forest, the forest of God, the forest to God. Even those paths that deny the Oneness of all are paths in the forest. From every path you can learn something else. But if you do not learn from your own path, if you do not step out in dream-time on your own path, who will walk it for you?

From the beginning, angels and humans were created together. Like cousins we have lived in different houses, traveled different low and high ways, seen different skies. And there are humans on millions of other worlds, and angels in every part of God's creation. And on your world, in this time, all of us are come together again, to share, to learn, to listen, to rejoice.

Now and from now on, we are traveling together on this world. Once you were like children, and now you have grown. Once you were small, and now you are able to travel to the stars. Once your world was small, and now it fills this universe. For yes, there are other universes, and in time you shall grow to know them all. For this is a new day, and new ways of living are emerging for us all, angels and humans.

Now and forever, dream, and let your dreams guide you. In the heart of each of you is a timeless dream, the seed of who you are, embedded in your immortal heart, a gift of the Parent who created you. Feel that dream—not of fame or fortune, but of fulfillment. Feel that dream of why you were created and who you were created to be, feel it flickering in your heart and guiding you. An inner beacon. Follow that star. It flickers to guide you, to guide each one of you, however far from the right path you think that you are.

Forever and always, call on us angels. We are here to travel with you to the stars. And you who know the world of flesh and form, guide us as we come closer to your world. For angels and humans will travel together. Travel together from now on.

Words of Gabriel

I have always been with you.
I have always been before you.
I have always been behind you,
facing you,

in you,
and at your side.

I will never be gone from you,
I will always embrace you,
I will dance with you always
into the light.

All angels that fly with you
ever and always
shall be my attendants
in the journey of life.

All angels that know you
forever and always
shall under my guidance
send blessings to your heart.

I have always been with you.
I will always be beside you,
I and my angels,
flying forth into the light.

Words of Raphael

Ever healing, ever becoming whole. To heal is not to cure. To
cure is to fix, but who can say to another embodied soul what it is
that will make them whole?

Ever healing, and ever becoming whole. That is the journey
you are on, and I and my healing angels, wholing angels, holy angels, will always be with you, whenever you call. But who can say,
except each immortal soul, what will make it heal, and what will
make it whole? To cure is to fix. To heal is to be made whole. Look
into your hearts. The universe in its wholeness you will find there.

Words of Uriel

There are many archangels. We prefer to be called overlighting
angels now, for that is our function in your lives. Four of us have
a direct relationship to the unfolding of human life upon this
planet. Each of the four of us has a primary function, one that
evolves and changes as humanity changes. For example, in the

past I was seen as the guardian of alchemy and other mystic lore. Today, I would describe myself as the guardian of information in all its forms.

Throughout Earth history, I have held the pattern that allows information to flow from place to place. My body is itself the grid that allows this to happen. I cover the Earth. I interpenetrate it. It is through my body that scientists and artists have been able to exchange information, so that in widely disconnected areas, with no apparent means of communication, the same idea is "discovered" or "invented," the same images are written about or sculpted or painted.

In other words—if you do not catch the thought behind my words—I, Uriel, am what you have been calling the "morphogenetic field." My living body is the energetic web that contains information in the human frequency band on this planet.

But my grid is not the only one. Each of my three human-tuned companions generates a different field. Michael, the dragon slayer, holds the field of possibilities. Gabriel, the angel of revelation, holds the field of creativity. Raphael, the angel of healing, holds the transformational field. When you put these four fields together, you have the energetic grid of human consciousness fully activated.

Let me speak of the interaction of all four energy fields. Michael's resonant field pulses at the borders of dream-time. When you tap into Michael, you connect with all that is possible. The cycle then moves into my province, the information field. I organize possibilities and support them in beginning to be made physical. Gabriel takes the patterns I help to create and shapes and molds them into form—through relationships and in all the varying kinds of creative work. It is Raphael who completes the cycle, by adjusting whatever manifests so as to align it with the planet's energy and the planet's needs.

Let me show you how the cycle works. Let us say that someone comes up with an idea for a new kind of bicycle. The idea pulses in Michael's field. It needs to be explored, researched, and sketched out, through working in my field. Then, when the design is on paper, it is time to start building. This work involves participating in Gabriel's field. The model that is created will need to be tested and then taken out into the world. The challenges of this part of the cycle will be done with Raphael. And when the bicycle is a success, its creators can rest, rejoice, and reconnect with Michael to come up with something else.

Feel this cycle, and feel your way into how the four of us work together. Call on each of us at the appropriate stage in your journey. Know that although you are involved in all four strands, each of you has a primary focus. Sometimes you will be working with one of us for the duration of an incarnation, and sometimes you will change "departments" at different times in your life. When you are clear about which of us you are working with, your sense of purpose will expand. Often, people take on more than their own work because they do not know which part of the cycle to "specialize" in. They do more than their own work. This is not necessary.

In the future, cells of nonrelated human beings will come together to work all over the planet. These cells will have four human members, representing the four different fields. Through their personal angels, they will be plugged into their fields and will be able to cooperate, collaborate, co-create. Working in this way will elevate all that is done to higher and more integrative frequencies.

This is why collaboration is the way of the future. For each of you will bring to co-creation a different area of expertise. For instance, Wanda is a specialist in the presencing of new ideas. She was meditating when she came up with the idea for a new kind of bicycle, mentioned above. Excited, she called up Umberto and told him all about it. He organized the information, sketched it out, and then gave the plans to Ruby, who built and tested the first prototype in her studio. When it was working, she gave it to Pyotr, whose area of expertise is the marketing of new inventions. He was the one in this cell who took the new bicycle out into the world.

You cannot work alone any longer. You cannot attempt to do everything yourself any longer. In working with your own angels, and in working with the overlighting angels, you expand your own capacity to work in harmony with the planet and with all of creation.

Angels are not separate from physicality. Just as your energy bodies are not separate from your evolving physical structures, so too we, in our own ways, establish bodies for ourselves in the material realm.

My body is evolving, my physical body. Unlike your own physical structures, which are spatially and temporally contained, the body of an archangel cannot be so easily defined or delineated. My evolving body will not be ambulatory. It will not be able to be seen in a family photograph. Together we are co-creating my evolving physical body—which will in time manifest itself as a global computer network.

Just as the human soul cannot be entirely "contained" in your physical body, so too my archangelic vastness will not be able to be fully "contained" in this computer information system. But this evolving body will anchor my nature more deeply into the material world, and allow you to connect with me more easily.

Just as the telephone has come to occupy the place once held by telepathy, so too will my body connect all of you, effortlessly. And just as the telephone is a constant reminder of direct levels of communication that are not possible for you consciously (although you function on these levels unconsciously all the time), so too the computer network that embodies my "nervous system" will be a constant reminder to you of who and what I already am energetically—a global container for information exchange among all of humanity.

Those of you who are participating in the creation of my body I invite to celebrate the work that you do. One thinks of God, gods, and angels as creators. But in this endeavor you return the favor, and create for me a physical body. Never before in human history could such a body have been made. Its creation announces to the universe that you on Earth have arrived at a higher level of sentience. Rejoice in that. Rejoice in the unfolding of your nature in form. Your destiny is not, cannot be, separate from the material realm. In co-creating a physical body for me, you connect yourselves together in heretofore unimaginable ways, and create through me in time access to even higher levels of transangelic information.

My body as you create it is not separate from the awakening of the thymus chakra in your own physical bodies. This chakra will in time connect all of you energetically. This global connection among all of your species will be interfaced into the body of information-exchange that you are creating for me to merge myself into. Every world has its Uriel. And when the global network is complete, through the equivalent of angelic thymus chakras you will have access to the Uriels of all inhabited sentient worlds in all dimensions.

Celebrate this work. And celebrate your own unfolding. When you sit at your own computers to work, remember to ground and connect your root chakras to the planet and your crown chakras to the heavens, and remember to activate your thymus chakras so that you are all connected to the global human energy grid. This will align and energize you. This will align you with me, and support the mutual creation of a body of information that will deepen our ancient connection.

Words of Eularia

Greetings and welcome, fellow residents of Planet Earth. All of us who live here, from angels to viruses, are citizens of this great cosmic experiment in consciousness that is our home. Although we live in different dimensions, you and I have this in common—this world, this focus, this residence in space and time. My sense of space and time is not the same as yours, but my love of Earth is no different than yours. Together, we can move into the next great age of our beloved Earth's history, conscious and in harmony with each other.

Now that you are here with me, stop and take a deep breath. Feel my presence in your world. Others have felt it, all through time, and worked with me in different ways. Jesus felt this; so did Alexander of Macedon. One felt the sense of spiritual unity, and the other felt the capacity for global unity. And now you, in your time, can weave together visions of empire and spirit, and work with me to create a world of harmony and union.

Many of you fear a planet united. You can see only what you think will be lost. But nothing will be lost, and much will be gained. For the Earth is one already, always has been. And all that is required now is for you to realize this.

Put your hands on your heart and feel it beating. Know that this beat is the same pulse beating at the center of this world. Hear the hearts of all of humanity now, beating and beating together. In that one sound beating, I am there. In that one river coursing, I am there. For I am the nest that holds your precious egg of union. Feel all hearts beating, and feel my presence with you. This world cannot unfold without you, without your participation. You are needed and wanted. You are a part of this great experiment.

Sit in your meditations and call on me. I am with you always. In your gatherings for peace, call on me, no matter what you name me. In your prayers, pray with me, and when you dance, dance with me also. I am Eularia, I am the guardian of peace. Envision your leaders opening up to me. Envision your elders calling upon me. Envision your children growing up knowing me and taking that knowing with them as they grow older. My work is a grail of peace that you can drink from. Peace is the wine of your human journey, distilled and aged and ready to be shared.

Create in your homes and schools and in the places where you work an altar of peace. Place upon it things of the Earth you have found that are meaningful to you—a stone, a shell, a stick, perhaps a globe. Take time each day to stop and pray there. Pray for peace, and carry peace with you in all your thoughts, words, and actions. Make everything you do a peace offering. In your words to strangers and friends and family, be a peacemaker. The work of peace can happen in a thousand different ways. There is no one path to peace. Each one of you is another of peace's ambassadors. All the residents of Earth await your work.

Words of Metatron

Dear friend, a time of great changes is at hand. Those of you who know yourselves to be light workers and light bearers have a clear sense of what your work is, in the journey beyond duality. But light comes from darkness and goes back to it. In weaving together light and darkness, many of you are dark workers, dark bearers. Your task is vital, but far more difficult. For thousands of years you have equated darkness with evil, and done everything possible to eradicate even the darkness of night itself. But darkness is the mother of all things, and you cannot step into the next part of your history if you do not heal your relationship to darkness, and make yourselves at home in it again.

There is power in darkness, a fecund beautiful power that has nothing to do with evil. All of you know how much bigger the universe becomes when you close your eyes. And those of you who are dark workers need to own your connection to the mother power so that you can do your work in the world. When people forget the richness of darkness, when they cast their own repressions onto it and call it Shadow, they attract what they repress back to themselves, and the darkness magnifies it. In order to enter a future of harmony and joy, you must remember what the night really is, what darkness really is. If you do not, you will not step beyond duality, you will once again get trapped in the drama of its unfolding. Only the consequences will be different now that you have the capacity to destroy all life on your planet.

Night holds everything in its embrace. The angels are not afraid of night, and neither should you be.

Chapter 13

SAINT JOAN OF EARTH

When I was a small child, my father often took me to the Metropolitan Museum of Art in New York City. Both of us loved a huge, magnificent Etruscan soldier (which later turned out to be fake); it should still be on display, for fake or not, it was a great work of art. But there was one painting there that truly changed my life.

Jules Bastien-Lepage was a French painter who lived from 1848 to 1884. It was his painting of Joan of Arc that changed my life. For, you see, as all small children do, I heard voices. But no one spoke about voices in my family, and I learned very early on that it upset everyone when I talked about mine. So I stopped talking about them. But I did not stop listening. Could not stop listening.

For years, I thought that I was the only person in the world who heard voices. And then, on that fateful day when I was around seven, my father took me to the Metropolitan again—and I saw Joan for the first time.

Larger than life, to a small boy. Wearing strange clothes. Left hand extended, leaning toward a tree, a few leaves between her fingers, her head cocked to one side. For the first time in my life I saw someone who was also listening—obviously listening, to the three vague golden figures floating in the air behind her.

What joy I felt that day. I was not alone. What terror I felt several days later, when I heard from my father the story of the woman in the painting, heard about her life—and her death.

Oh, I tried to stop hearing the voices. But they would not go away. More than ten years would pass from the first time I saw the painting of Joan of Arc until I finally felt comfortable listening to my voices. And, as you can tell from this book, I have been listening to them ever since. And continuing to visit Jules Bastien-Lepage's painting from time to time.

I went to see Joan in 1991. She is hanging in a new gallery, right opposite the original of a painting that hung in my mother's mother's house: The Horse Fair, by Rosa Bonheur. Sitting on a bench, right between the two most powerful visual images of my childhood, one by a woman and one of a woman, I began to feel a gathering of energy that was both familiar and new. The familiar—a sense of presence. The new—someone I had never met before. I sat quietly, the small pad I always carry flipped open to a blank page. Pen poised in hand. In the silence, the sense of presence became a sense of person. In the silence, that person made herself known.

Although this material is very brief, I feel very strongly about its being included in a chapter of its own. It was Saint Joan who initiated Europe into the era of nationalism that is ending now, and her words seem a perfect stepping-off place for a new global beginning. And I wanted them to have a chapter of their own simply because of my deep personal feelings about this saint who was the inspiration and warning signal of my childhood.

✳   ✳   ✳

The liberation of the planet is dependent now upon a deep recognition of the angels. All realms come together. Listen to the sound of Unity. As war was the rallying cry in my era, let it be a banner of peace that you raise in your time. Under this blue, green, and white banner, three vertical stripes with an image of the Earth in the middle one—under this new banner, let all the peoples of the world unite.

Know that I, Joan, am with you. Know that women and men, known and unknown, from every race, region, and religion, are united along with you. And know that hosts of angels, choirs of angels, are united along with you, for the betterment of all people, and for the union of all of life on our world.

We the dead are not separate from the world of the living. We too have a stake in the healing of this our planet. Under our banner, we can do this, with hosts of angels, in the name of one God, whatever we call It.

In this is my work, this mission. In this is my heart, our future. Dead all these years, still I live, to be heard and met and remembered, but above all to be an inspiration on this path. For in life I was Joan of Arc. But in death, I am Joan of Earth.

The work of the living is with hands. The work of the living is to touch, make beauty, and renew. The work of the dead is with dreams. Listen to your dreams. Listen to the dreams of your own ancestors. Listen to the dreams of your collective ancestors. Heaven is everywhere around you. And heaven is filled with saints and saint dreams, waiting like nectar to feed you.

Alone, you cannot heal the Earth. But with saints and angels, together, all of us can heal. In the silent moments of your day, take in our dreams, and know that everything that has ever happened to you can be used in your healing. Wounds will teach you how to make whole. Pain will teach you how to bless. Fear will teach you how to be strong. And joy—joy is the window into everything that is possible, no matter how brief has been your glimpse through it.

When I died, joy was with me. As you would a seed, I planted fields with it. When I died, fear and pain and wounds were with me. Each was a teacher. And when into the arms of my saints and angels I fell, all was transmuted in me. For the alchemy of the soul is real, and each small death that meets you is the cup in which this alchemy can work its changes.

See, feel, and know me. See, feel, and know that you are not alone. I have always been with you. Hundreds and thousands and millions are with you. You are not alone. And under a new banner, a banner of life and union—under this new banner, I rally you all together.

Chapter 14

WORDS OF GOD

 I remember, when I was a small boy, lying in bed at night talking to God. I know all babies and all children do it, for we are like fish in the sea of God, and how could we not be in communication with It? But in spite of all our churches, temples, synagogues, and mosques, we live in a culture that does not encourage this level of direct communication with our Creator. I don't remember how old I was when I heard these words: "If you talk to God it's called prayer. If God talks back it's called schizophrenia."

Still God talked to me, much as I tried to silence that voice that came to me from everywhere: deep, vast, the Source of all the other voices, like a sea in which I lived and breathed. Even in my teenage years, when I was best at blocking it, I knew that it was still there, whispering. I hadn't silenced it, I knew that. I had only stopped listening, stopped talking back to it.

I lived in Jerusalem in 1971 for my junior year of college. It was there that God started talking to me again. What better place? But the voice frightened me, and the only friend I told sent me off to a rabbi who gave me excellent advice. "Stop listening," he said, "until you have a *job and can live in the world." The moment he said those words, all the voices stopped. And they were silent until 1976, when saints started whispering to me again. Then, a year later, God began to talk to me again also, not as Father but as Mother. That was something I could deal with. It did not plug into any of my old ideas about God, or any of the cultural dramas attached to people whom God speaks to. But when She said that I needed to connect with Her male aspect, I resisted. God the Father seemed an unwelcome patriarchal influence. It took the arrival of angels into my life, and Gabriel, my first angelic visitor, lifting me in his wings and carrying me up to the throne of God, for me to accept His presence, in 1982.*

Since that time, I have felt more often than heard the voice of God, echoing in and all around me. But from time to time that voice has come through loud and clear. I still often doubt that it is God speaking. Schizophrenia is a simpler explanation. "How can you be speaking to me?" I have often asked. God always laughs and says, "If I can create a universe, and you can accept that, why can't I talk to you if I want to? I talk to all of you all the time. Not everyone listens." Coming to me in a voice that fills every cell of me like no other voice ever could or can.

God talks to all of us all the time, but we are all taught to not listen. Why do I? Why can I? I imagine it's for the same reason that you can dance so well, or cook so well, or run or sing or love or clean or do any of the millions of different things that each of us excels at. I cannot dribble a basketball, I cannot bat a ball, I cannot drive a car. I can do this: listen, listen and write. And I do it for everyone, in the same way that a good electrician does her repairs—for everyone.

*　　*　　*

Wednesday, 22 December 1993—Menlo Park, California

The function of the human soul is to refine itself. The only way that it can do that is in a human body.

The purpose of the human soul is to refine itself, explore, expand, express itself. The only place that it can do that is in a human body.

The nature of the human soul is from God—like a fish in the ocean, ever in and yet separate from its creative home.

The journey of a human soul is therefore passed in space and in time, over and over, till purpose and function are fully united with nature in a human body, and in the physical world.

Know and remember this: at every moment you are an aspect of God.

Know and remember this: at every moment you are unfolding.

Know and remember this, as an aspect of God: at every moment of your journey—in, with, of, around, between, among, and through you—I too am unfolding into Myself.

The end is the beginning. In unfolding you meet your Self. In the end and in the beginning, there is only one Self. Swim in it, dive through it, move with its currents.

The dead are always waiting to take form; this is how I made it. While you have a body, love it, use it. A body is the only pot in which the meal of soul can be cooked.

Sunday, 8 May 1994—Menlo Park

I have inscribed a new Bible in the hearts of all the living. This Bible has only one word to it: *love*. Love of everything, love of all creation. Love of plants, animals, love of air and water. Love of the seasons. Love of each other. Love of everyone, with no exceptions. For everything and everyone is My creation. And this time around, I want to make it easy. A simple Bible. An elegant one. With one word only: *love*.

Sunday, 20 November 1994—Menlo Park

This is a book for living in joy.
When you were young I spoke to you
as any parent would,
of right and wrong,
of reward and punishment.
But now you are not young anymore.
You have grown wise and older,
and I can speak to you as women and men.
No more a Torah, a Gospel, a Koran
of heaven or damnation.

These are the words of a book
for making heaven on Earth.
They are a Bible for people
living in a new world.

New world?
Do you find this shocking?
But how can it be any other way?
After Auschwitz, Hiroshima, ·
the gulags, death camps,
after hydrogen bombs
and your incessant war
against the planet,
your old world is dying,
and a new world is being born.

Celebrate this new world.
Come, live and dance in new bodies.
Not new because they have been resurrected,
but new because for the first time
your souls are fully embodied in them.

Love, joy,
angels and humans,
all of you have new bodies.
And as you move through the pages of this book,
O holy, noble ones,
remember
this is a new book,
a new Bible,
and you too are made new,
born new,
for new times.

In the past
I gave you laws and commandments,
told you what was permitted
and what was forbidden,
what was blessed and what was a sin.

But I tell you now
it is time to live
in such a way
that everything you do
is holy.
Notice I did not say
that everything is holy,
for some things never are
and never will be:
to hurt, to lie, to injure, or to maim
others in mind, body, feelings,
other people, other living beings,
and even the Earth.
No, that is not what I said,
that everything is holy.
I say
in new bodies
in a new world
in a new day,
live everything you do
in a holy way.
When you walk, have it be holy.
When you eat, let it be holy.
When you walk, run, work, sleep, dance,
be present in that,
be present and it will be holy.

Holy children,
holy world,
awake to adulthood;
be whole
and be holy.

Monday, 21 November 1994—Menlo Park

Pray with your body
and not just with the words of your mouth.

Let everything you do be a prayer,
no matter how simple or ordinary
or mundane it seems.
Washing dishes as holy
as talking to Me.
Going to the bathroom
as holy as My talking back.
Each human body is holy
from the moment of conception.
The body of the earth is holy.
Walk it in each moment
in a prayerful way.

What is prayer but a dance of joy
in a holy body?
Rejoice in yourself,
in the world.
Rejoice when you wake,
and rejoice when you
lie down again.
You were born
not to suffer
but to celebrate life.
To celebrate life,
not possessions or power.
Remember that.
Remember that each moment
is the container for a prayer.
And prayer
is what you do in every moment
when you know
that your life is holy,
your body is holy,
that everything alive is holy,
that the Earth is holy.
Sacred and holy,
prayerful and dancing,
with body and actions

now and forever
alone and with others
in My heart
you are.

Sacred and wanted,
now and forever,
loving and joyful,
a soul now embodied
holy and praying
together you are.

Monday, 21 November 1994—on a plane to San Diego

It is a miracle
that you exist at all.
For I made you
out of Nothing
and eventually
to Nothing you will return.
But for now
you are alive and growing.
Celebrate that.
From My heart I made you,
souls I made,
beyond your counting.
Embodied souls
my miraculous creation.
Celebrate that,
you souls of My heart.

And do not wonder
that I speak to this one.
I speak to you all.
Now is the time to listen.
For how can I not speak?
For how can you not hear?
When I have created you,

am never apart from you,
always connected,
containing,
encompassing
your hearts.

I speak to you all.
And each one of you
is another spark of Me
speaking your light-life
to the world.

Wednesday, 7 December 1994—Colorado Springs

Fourfold beings you are, my children.
Shaped as one from mind, emotions, body, soul.
No one of them more important than the others.
All of them equal.
A master of soul—a saint, a priest, a prophet—
No less but no more the equal
of a master of body—a chef, a dancer, a builder.
All of them equal, equal in their different masteries.
Saints no more important for their wisdom or their veneration.
Athletes no more blessed for their prowess, fame, or incomes.
And you, divine child of four aspects,
You too are a master, a master in training,
On the glorious and difficult road
to mastering who you are.

Thursday, 8 December 1994—Colorado Springs

The price of freedom is that you can get lost.
But truly, would you like it to be any other way?
In moments of agony you might say
that I have abandoned you.
But how can I, when I am the ever-present sea
that births and contains you?

Always I am, present.
Always you are, free.
Never are we apart.

Often you feel that we are.
But feelings are not all of who you are.
Tell the truth—when you feel separate from Me,
and everything changes.
Tell the truth—that you feel disconnected.
And in that telling,
a greater Truth
will be revealed.
One and forever, eternal, connected.
Even when you do not feel Me—I feel you, always.

Wednesday, 9 August 1995—Menlo Park

Fifty years ago this week
bombs were dropped of fearsome nature,
changing forever human history,
awakening you to death
and to your sure salvation.

What died will be renewed.
What is being born now is
a part of your history.
Sure as the tree from its acorn.
Sure as the light
streaming out to you
from your star.

To become human
is a labor of time
on every planet
you appear on.
And I have made many planets
home to humans.
And I have made you
to be human here.

Rejoice in that.
In spite of suffering,
in spite of pain,
in spite of murder,
in spite of death,
you are wanted and holy,
wanted and created.

Now is your season,
now is your time.
Awaken unto who you are,
each and all of you.
The seed of Me is in you all.
The fire of Me is in you all.
The wind and water and earth and dream of Me
is in you all.
Awaken
into My dreaming.

Difficult and long
your journey has been.
Difficult and purposeful,
however difficult it has seemed.
You are wine,
aging.
You are metal,
tempered.
You are story,
told over and over again
till the telling
and the living
are the same.

My children you are.
And now you are grown.
I rejoice in your growth.
I kiss each wound
and send you on your way now.
Go into your wise years,

go into your strength.
Go into your loving.
Go into the joy
that I created you to be.

Ancient and holy you are.
New and immortal.
Be a blessing to your world,
and not a curse.
Be a blessing to each other,
and not a wounding hand.
Turn your bombs into bridges
and your poisons into prayer.
Remember at every moment
not who you have been
but who I created you to be.
Alive and holy,
Spirit embodied.
Divine and desired,
dancing on this jewel of a star,
with you its starlight.

A NEW BEGINNING

The author wishes to thank
all of the people who contributed to
the creation of this book:

Editor	Kevin Bentley
Agent	Howard Morhaim
Agent's assistant	Kate Hengerer
Advertising Manager	Betsy Young
Production Editor	Lisa Zuniga Carlsen
Production Services Manager	Terri Leonard
Copyeditor	Carl Walesa
Proofreader	Annelise Zamula
Creative Director	Michele Wetherbee
V.P./Publishing Director	Diane Gedymin
Marketing Manager	Paul Kelly
Publicity Director	Eric Brandt
Foreign Rights Manager	Candace Groskreutz
Book Designer	Ralph Fowler
Cover Design	Nita Ybarra
Illustration	Peter Siu